PROJECT AIR FORCE

T0170133

Using RAND's Military Career Model to Evaluate the Impact of Institutional Requirements on the Air Force Space Officer Career Field

Alexander D. Rothenberg, Lisa M. Harrington, Paul Emslie, Tara L. Terry

Prepared for the United States Air Force

For more information on this publication, visit www.rand.org/t/RR1302

Library of Congress Cataloging-in-Publication Data is available for this publication.
ISBN: 978-0-8330-9656-2

Published by the RAND Corporation, Santa Monica, Calif.
© Copyright 2017 RAND Corporation
RAND® is a registered trademark.

Support RAND
Make a tax-deductible charitable contribution at
www.rand.org/giving/contribute

www.rand.org

Preface

In recent years, filling all manpower authorization requirements for U.S. Air Force career fields has become increasingly difficult. These requirements include not only operational and staff positions that support mission demands, but also additional requirements levied on career fields. *Institutional requirements* (IRs) are one source of these additional requirements. IRs are valid, funded manpower requirements—such as for recruiters, instructors, generalist staff officers, or operational support—that do not align with a traditional, functional career field but are needed to support the Air Force institution.

For career field managers, IRs compete with operational requirements for the same pool of manpower. IRs also affect the career development of individual officers. In some cases, the experience provided by an IR assignment contributes to an officer's competitiveness for future assignments and promotion. Other IR positions are considered side tracks that keep officers from obtaining additional depth in their operational specialty. Some career field managers, such as managers in the space and cyber fields, believe the impact of IRs on manning and career development is serious enough to warrant formal study.

Air Force leadership in the offices of the Deputy Chief of Staff, Operations and the Deputy Chief of Staff, Manpower, Personnel, and Services asked RAND Project AIR FORCE to examine the Air Force's IRs and help determine whether there is a better way to source, manage, and man these service needs. The Air Force also asked RAND to develop a method to assess the impact of IRs on the ability to fill career field core positions and apply this methodology to the space career field.

This report describes our assessment of the impact of IRs on the space career field. It presents a methodology by which to conduct such an assessment and reports our findings of IRs' impact on space officer manning and individual officer development. The research was conducted within the Manpower, Personnel, and Training Program of RAND Project AIR FORCE.

RAND Project AIR FORCE

RAND Project AIR FORCE (PAF), a division of the RAND Corporation, is the U.S. Air Force's federally funded research and development center for studies and analyses. PAF provides the Air Force with independent analyses of policy alternatives affecting the development, employment, combat readiness, and support of current and future air, space, and cyber forces. Research is conducted in four programs: Force Modernization and Employment; Manpower, Personnel, and Training; Resource Management; and Strategy and Doctrine. The research reported here was prepared under contract FA7014-06-C-0001.

Additional information about PAF is available on our website:
http://www.rand.org/paf/

This report documents work originally shared with the U.S. Air Force on July 15, 2015. The draft report, issued on October 27, 2015, was reviewed by formal peer reviewers and U.S. Air Force subject-matter experts.

Contents

Preface..iii

Figures..vii

Tables..viii

Summary..ix

Acknowledgments..xii

Abbreviations..xiii

1. Introduction..1

    Organization of Document..2

2. Calibrating the Military Career Model..3

    Background..3

    Steady-State Modeling..4

    Specifying Jobs...6

    Acquisition Jobs..10

    Operations and Staff Jobs...11

        Intelligence, Surveillance, and Reconnaissance...14

        Satellite Systems..15

        Space Control...16

        Space Staff...17

        Space Test...18

        Space Warfare Command and Control Operations..19

        Spacelift...19

        Space Warning...20

        Missile Defense Staff Jobs...21

    IR Job Group..21

    Education and Development Job Group..24

    Summary...24

3. Results: Reducing the Number of IR Positions...26

    Baseline Results..26

        End Strength and Grade Distribution...26

        Retention..27

        Average Fill Rates of Jobs..28

    Changing IRs: Results Overview...32

    Detailed Results: IR Reduction of 50 Percent...38

        Changes in Fill Rates of Different Types of Jobs..38

    Effects on Individuals...41

        Retention Patterns for Officers with Different Types of IR Experiences....................42

        Diversity of Officer Experiences..43

Tables

1.1. IR Jobs by Job Group and Air Force Identifier... 1

2.1. Fill Priorities 8

2.2. Acquisition Job Characteristics.. 10

2.3. Operations Job Characteristics: ISR 14

2.4. Staff Job Characteristics: ISR 14

2.5. Operations Job Characteristics: Satellite Systems 15

2.6. Staff Job Characteristics: Satellite Systems 16

2.7. Operations Job Characteristics: Space Control... 16

2.8. Staff Job Characteristics: Space Control... 17

2.9. Operations Job Characteristics: Space Staff 17

2.10. Staff Job Characteristics: Space Staff 18

2.11. Operations Job Characteristics: Space Test 18

2.12. Staff Job Characteristics: Space Test.. 18

2.13. Operations Job Characteristics: Space Warfare C2 19

2.14. Staff Job Characteristics: Space Warfare C2 19

2.15. Operations Job Characteristics: Spacelift 20

2.16. Staff Job Characteristics: Spacelift 20

2.17. Operations Job Characteristics: Space Warning 21

2.18. Staff Job Characteristics: Space Warning.. 21

2.19. Staff Job Characteristics: Missile Defense 21

2.20. IR Job Characteristics 23

2.21. Education and Development Job Characteristics.. 24

2.22. Summary of Authorizations and Positions, FY 2014 and Steady State.................... 25

A.1. Previous IR Experiences: Statistics on Employment Periods.................................... 48

Summary

An *institutional requirement* (IR) is a U.S. Air Force manpower requirement needed to support the Air Force institution, including positions like recruiters, instructors, or political-military affairs specialists. These positions may not align well with traditional functional career fields. Generally, IRs do not have to be filled by officers with a particular specialty or from a particular career field, so various career fields are "taxed" to fill them. Career field assignment teams then assign officers to fill IR positions allocated to their career field. Typically, however, some IRs go unfilled because career fields have a limited pool of officers to fill both IR positions and core career field authorizations. In these situations, the additional stress that IRs place on some career fields is significant.

In fiscal year 2014, RAND Project AIR FORCE was asked to carry out research on IR processes and impacts. In this document, we summarize our findings from modeling the effect of filling IR positions on a career field's health, given that filling IR positions draws labor away from core authorizations. We adapted RAND's Military Career Model (MCM), a detailed personnel simulation model, to evaluate the impact of changes to IRs on the space officer (13S) career field. The model enabled us to study how IRs affect a variety of career field metrics, including the ability to simultaneously fill core requirements and IR positions. We also examined how changing the number of IRs affects the operational development, career experience diversity, and career paths of space officers.

Effects of IRs on the Space Career Field

Generally, we found that the fill rates of most space jobs would not be affected by reductions in the total number of IRs allocated to the space career field. The highest-priority space career field positions would nearly always be filled, even if the field provided more IR positions than it currently does. Jobs with lower priority than IR positions often require grades and experiences inapplicable to IR positions and therefore also would be unaffected by a change in IR requirements. If fewer IRs were assigned to the space career field, the biggest impact would be on jobs with slightly less priority than IR positions, particularly staff jobs at major commands and headquarters at the grade of O-4. Taken together, this evidence suggests that IRs have a substantial numerical impact on space career field manning, but this impact is limited to a subset of positions.

Effects of IRs on Space Officers

The experiences of individual officers in the space career field are often used as examples of the negative effects of IRs on officer careers, including effects on operational depth, diversity of experience across the space enterprise, and career advancement. Our review of the simulated officers in the MCM showed little evidence of these negative outcomes with respect to experience diversity or the number of operational tours filled by officers. We did find, however, that some individuals who were assigned to IR positions would otherwise have filled detachment commander positions (generally viewed as priority, career-enhancing jobs) or joint staff officer positions (which get mixed reviews on importance and officer development). On the other hand, some IR positions, such as executive officer and aide-de-camp, potentially positively influence career development and progression, as selection is competitive and selectees have opportunities to observe senior leader decisionmaking, gain exposure across functional areas, and undergo mentoring.

Being assigned to an IR position has the potential for both positive and negative effects on officer development and career progression. Because of these potential impacts, those involved in assigning officers need to be attentive to the careers of individual officers in subspecialties that need particular operational experiences and those with the potential for senior staff and command positions. Personnel officers also need to be attentive to situations where IRs offer experiences and competencies that, while different than those of space jobs, are of similar career value.[1]

Recommendations

While IRs do divert manpower that could be used to fill space officer positions, IRs do not compete with all types of space positions for officers. Therefore, careful management in the following areas could lessen the effects of filling IRs on the career field.

- **Increase the fidelity of priorities for space jobs and ensure space officer assignments are made based on these priorities.** Our analysis of the impacts of IRs at the career field and individual level revealed the importance of prioritizing jobs. The space career field manager should consider creating a prioritization scheme with more levels (similar perhaps to the *must-fill*; *priority-fill, high*; *priority-fill, low*; and *entitlement-fill* ratings used in our analysis). Top-to-bottom career field visibility of job priorities—from space senior leaders to the space assignment team—will also help ensure that all high-priority positions are filled.
- **Carefully select IR jobs for space officers.** For individual space officers, IRs have some degree of impact on diversity of career experiences and depth of operational experience and can represent lost opportunities. As a result, the space officer assignment team should seek IR positions that provide officers with experiences and competencies to enhance and

---

[1] A companion report (Harrington et al., 2017) addresses how IR positions are allocated to each career field and provides recommendations for improving the number, distribution, and prioritization of IR positions for the Air Force broadly and for individual career fields.

complement their space expertise, rather than continuing the current practice of seeking positions for which officers might be likely to volunteer.

- **Continue to maintain and possibly expand the use and management of the Space Experience Code (SPEC).** This code, which categorizes positions into subcategories in the 13S career field, was invaluable to the modeling conducted for this study. Without these codes, identifying types of positions below the Air Force Specialty Code (AFSC) level is difficult. Air Force Space Command should consider extending the use of the SPEC from labeling personnel with particular experiences to labeling each space authorization with a SPEC so that job-level analyses can be performed in the future. In addition, we recommend that the Deputy Chief of Staff, Manpower, Personnel, and Services investigate the development of a similar standardized coding scheme that could be used by all officer career fields to code authorizations to allow for analyses of position types within AFSCs.

The use of the MCM and the resulting analysis presented in this report are a first step toward understanding the impact of IRs on the space career field. Future work could examine the impact of alternative approaches to filling IR positions—by, for example, examining the effect of changing the priority assigned to space officer and IR positions. The methodology can be readily used to study the impact of IRs on other career fields as well. We recommend that future work evaluate the impact of IRs on multiple career fields to determine which career fields have the most to gain from an improved IR selection and allocation processes.

Acknowledgments

We are grateful to many people who were involved in this research. In particular, we would like to thank our Air Force sponsors, Maj Gen Martin Whelan, Deputy Chief of Staff, Operations, and Brig Gen Brian Kelly, Headquarters U.S. Air Force, Directorate of Military Force Policy, Force Management and Enterprise Readiness Analysis Division. In addition, we would like to thank the space career field manager and action officers who provided their functional expertise and guidance throughout this study: Col Stuart Pettis, Col Todd Diel, and Maj Jason Adams. This research would not have been possible without their contributions.

Many RAND colleagues contributed to this effort. Most importantly, Pete Schirmer's expertise and insights on the Military Career Model were key. The authors thank Al Robbert for his insights. We also want to thank our reviewers, James R. Hosek and Pete Schirmer, for their thoughtful comments that greatly improved this report.

Abbreviations

13S	space officer
AF/A1	Deputy Chief of Staff, Manpower, Personnel, and Services
AF/A1PF	Headquarters U.S. Air Force, Directorate of Military Force Policy, Force Management and Enterprise Readiness Analysis Division
AFIT	Air Force Institute of Technology
AFPC	Air Force Personnel Center
AFSC	Air Force Specialty Code
AFSPC	Air Force Space Command
AOC	area of concern
C2	command and control
Det/CC	detachment commander
FY	fiscal year
IDE	intermediate developmental education
IR	institutional requirement
ISR	intelligence, surveillance, and reconnaissance
MAJCOM	major command
MCM	Military Career Model
MPES	Manpower Programming and Execution System
NAF	numbered Air Force
SOAP	Space Officer Allocation Plan
SOPS	Satellite Operations Squadron
SPEC	Space Experience Code

1. Introduction

An *institutional requirement* (IR) is a manpower requirement needed to support the Air Force institution—such as recruiters, instructors, or political-military affairs specialists. These positions may not align well with functionally focused, traditional career field structures. Generally, IRs do not have to be filled by officers with a particular specialty or from a particular career field. Various career fields are "taxed" to fill IRs—that is, they are assigned a certain number of specific IR positions to fill. Career field assignment teams then assign officers to the allocated positions. However, some IR positions typically go unfilled because of the limited pool of officers to fill both IR positions and core career field authorizations. In these situations, the additional stress that IRs place on some career fields is significant. Table 1.1 lists the types of IRs that career fields are tasked to fill and shows how we mapped Air Force Special Duty or Reporting Identifiers into IR job groups.

Table 1.1. IR Jobs by Job Group and Air Force Identifier

Air Force Special Duty or Reporting Identifier	IR Job Title	IR Job Group
81T0	Instructor	Academic
82A0	Academic Program Manager	
80C0	U.S. Air Force Academy Cadet Squadron Commander	Accessions
81C0	Officer Training School Training Commander	
83R0	Recruiter	Recruiting
85G0	Honor Guard	
30C0	Support Commander	Functional Command
91C0	Commander	
88A0	Aide-de-Camp	Senior Leader Support
97E0	Executive Officer	
16GX	Operations Staff Officer	
16RX	Planning and Programming	
16FX	Regional Affairs Specialist	
16PX	Political-Military Affairs Specialist	Operations and Strategy
86M0	Operations Management	
86P0	Command and Control	
87XX	Inspections	

NOTE: This table shows the mapping between Air Force Special Duty or Reporting Identifiers into IR job groups, which we use for analysis purposes. Our research team determined these job groupings.

In fiscal year (FY) 2014, RAND Project AIR FORCE was asked to research IR processes and impacts. In this report, we summarize our findings from modeling the effect of filling IR positions on a career field's health, given that filling IR positions draws labor away from the core authorizations. We focused on the space officer (13S) career field, because it was a career field where personnel officers felt that IR positions were impacting their ability to fill other positions. We adapted RAND's Military Career Model (MCM), a detailed personnel simulation model, to evaluate the impact of IRs on a variety of career field metrics, including the ability of the career field to meet its core requirements and fill IR positions simultaneously. We also look at the impact on officers themselves, examining how changing the number of IR positions assigned to a career field affects the operational development, diversity of career experiences, and expertise of senior officers. In a companion report, we provide a more detailed overview of the process for filling IRs, as well as recommendations for improving IR manning and processes (Harrington et al., 2017).

Organization of Document

This document is organized into several chapters. The next chapter describes the MCM and how we calibrated various parameters of the model to the 13S career field. These parameters include positions, retention rates, promotion rates, and job characteristics, among others. Chapter Three describes the results of the modeling work. We first present baseline results, demonstrating that the baseline model matches various aspects of the 13S career field quite well. We next investigate what would happen to fill rates, manning, and officer development under several different scenarios. Chapter Four concludes with a summary and recommendations.

2. Calibrating the Military Career Model

This chapter provides a brief overview of RAND's MCM and describes how the model's inputs were calibrated to fit data collected for the 13S officer career field.

Background

The MCM allows researchers to examine the effects of different human capital management policies on a number of manpower outcomes. The model was originally developed to examine how changes to the Defense Officer Personnel Management Act of 1980 would affect career path alternatives (Schirmer et al., 2006). It was also later used as part of a project for the Office of the Secretary of Defense to examine the impact of the 2009 National Defense Authorization Act's proposed changes to general and flag officer requirements (Schirmer, 2009). Since then, the model has been adapted for a variety of military personnel applications (see O'Neill, 2012, and Nataraj et al., 2014). The model logic and code were recently migrated to Java, and several researchers have extended the capabilities of the original model.

The MCM is a vacancy-based simulation model, which creates simulated officers and runs over discrete time intervals. In each interval or period, the model's subroutines access new officers, assign existing officers to the current pool of jobs, and separate or retire other officers. During the assignment process, some officers will take training courses to advance their careers, some will be assigned to fill low-level jobs, and others will be assigned to more important positions after being promoted based on their grade and experience.

During the simulation, the model records the history of assignments, promotion, and retention for all simulated officers. From this detailed simulation data, it is possible to construct many different outputs to measure various aspects of career field health. These include the average fill rates of particular jobs, the grade structure of officers over time, the total end strength of the officer pool, retention curves, and more. By changing the parameters of the model to mimic policy changes and by examining the model outputs that result from such changes, researchers can study how specific policy changes may impact different aspects of a career field's health.[2]

In this report, we evaluate the effect of changes to IRs on the space officer career field. To do so, we examine different metrics to determine whether increasing or decreasing the number of IRs filled by space officers affects the ability of the career field to fill certain types of 13S jobs or

---

[2] Although the model operates at the individual level, with a sequence of assignments given to each simulated officer, the model is not equipped to make predictions about an actual individual's career; all individuals in the model are simulated and do not have exact real-world counterparts.

the diversity of experiences gained by officers in the career field. The following sections of this chapter provide an overview of the user-defined inputs and procedures of the MCM and discuss how those inputs were calibrated to data from the space career field.

Steady-State Modeling

The MCM simulates the behavior of a career field over a long time horizon, approximating the personnel system's steady state. In FY 2014, 1,522 officers were authorized to serve in a 13S duty billet. However, in practice, some core 13S officers serve in duty Air Force Specialty Codes (AFSCs) other than 13S, and some officers from other core specialties are in 13S positions. We expect that because of positive crossflow, there are more officers from other AFSCs serving in 13S positions than 13S officers serving in other AFSCs, so our net inventory number to fill 13S billets is probably much higher. To account for this, based on personnel data, we increased the model's total inventory number to 1,690 (a net gain of 168).

Because the model is a steady-state model of career field behavior, we made some choices regarding (1) accessions and (2) the grade distribution of officers and positions in the model. Accessions were chosen to ensure that the total inventory in the model approached the FY 2014 level of 1,690 every year. In FY 2014, the 13S community accessed 148 individuals, but this level of accessions is too low to sustain FY 2014 requirements. This means either that accessions need to be increased or greater crossflow is needed. If the number of accessions remains low, and the number of positions to be filled remains unchanged, we would expect an increase in the number of unfilled positions—first at the lower grades and, over time, in overall company-grade and field-grade manning.

Because we wanted to be able to isolate the effects of change in the number of IRs, we increased the 13S accessions in the model to a sustainment level of 180.[3] By making this choice, the simulation exercise allows us to understand what would happen if the FY 2014 inventory level of 1,690 was maintained for many years, approximating the steady-state behavior of the personnel system.[4]

The grade distribution of the FY 2014 13S inventory is shown in Figure 2.1 (blue bars), together with the modeled steady-state grade distribution (gray bars). Clearly, the FY 2014 grade distribution is unsustainable, as it implies a near 100-percent continuation rate between O-4 and O-5. Retention probabilities for core 13S officers, plotted in Figure 2.2, show that this is not the case. Retention rates in the figure were constructed using average annual separation rates by commissioned year of service data supplied by Headquarters U.S. Air Force, Directorate of

---

[3] In the MCM, time periods are quarters of a fiscal year. The model accessed 45 individuals in each time period, for a total of 180 individuals each year.

[4] This inventory level includes permanent party authorizations and student, trainee, and personnel positions.

Military Force Policy, Force Management and Enterprise Readiness Analysis Division (AF/A1PF).

In general, 13S officers have very high retention rates in their first four years due to initial service commitments. Rates drop significantly in year five, when they are first eligible to separate, and again in year eight, before consideration for promotion to major and after most officers have had two assignments.

Based on these retention probabilities and a sustainment level of authorizations, we obtained a steady-state total for modeled officers, plotted in Figure 2.1 (gray bars). The significantly increased proportion of O-3s is due to the fact that retention falls substantially in year seven of service, when officers are eligible to separate. In a steady state, there will be more O-3s than in FY 2014, because a large portion of them will separate. The steady-state inventory for the 13S career field is much more dominated by junior officers than the current distribution, which has a large portion of O-4s and O-5s.

Figure 2.1. Total 13S Officer Authorizations (FY 2014) and Modeled Officers

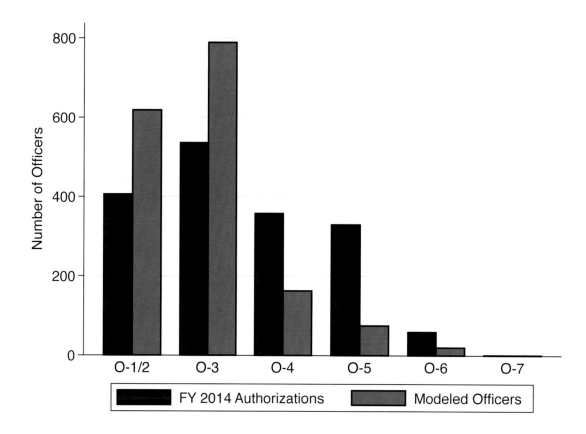

SOURCE: Air Force Personnel Center, Authorized Manpower Master File (MPW), September 1, 2014.

Figure 2.2. Core 13S Retention Probability by Commissioned Years of Service

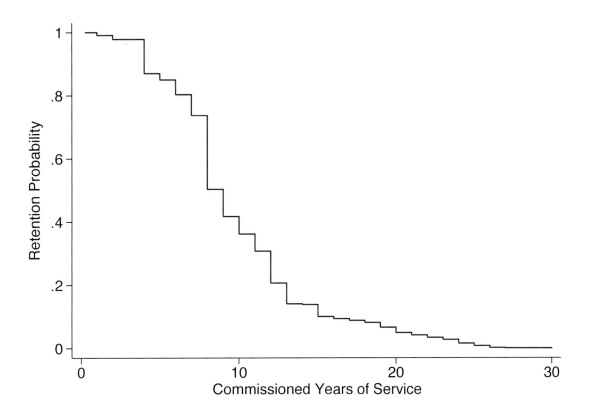

SOURCE: Headquarters U.S. Air Force, Directorate of Military Force Policy, Force Management and Enterprise Readiness Analysis Division, "Cumulative Continuation Rates for 13S Officers by Commissioned Years of Service," data files, 2015. This figure produces the Kaplan-Meier estimator of the retention probability of a 13S officer by commissioned year of service. The line is plotted as a step function, with a series of declining horizontal steps, because the value of the retention probabilities between successive steps is assumed to be constant.

Specifying Jobs

After determining the steady state distribution of 13S officers, we next turned to specifying the jobs, or position aggregates, held by space officers in the model. To do so, we first worked with data on positions, which are described in unit manpower documents. These data contain records of all positions in the Air Force and are populated with variables that identify the grade, AFSC, and other characteristics necessary to perform the duties of that particular position. The data also include information about the location of that position in a given unit or organization. Unit manpower documents are a part of the Manpower Programming and Execution System (MPES), a larger system for managing Air Force manpower resources.

Initially, we extracted all positions from FYs 2009 through 2014 that required an AFSC of 13S. In FY 2014, there were 1,562 such positions. To aggregate these positions in a way useful for the career field manager and to align with potential personnel policy changes, we coded each

6

position according to an identifier called the Space Experience Code (SPEC).[5] The SPEC was developed by Air Force Space Command (AFSPC) in 2004 to identify and track the experience that different types of positions in the space career field provide for space officers. It is used for personnel planning and management purposes (Hutto, 2004). We used the SPEC to map each of the 1,562 positions to a job type. There are 130 unique three-digit SPECs that can be used to categorize 13S positions. Using these codes and working with the sponsor, we further aggregated positions into 96 different jobs, spread across three job groups: acquisition, operations, and staff. The jobs in these job groups are described in detail in the next several sections of this chapter. After determining the set of jobs that officers could fill, we further calibrated the model by specifying information on the characteristics of those jobs. These characteristics determine whether individuals are eligible for a specific job, how long individuals can stay in a job, whether individuals are allowed to retire after holding the job, and the preferred and required experience for a job assignment.

To assign an officer to a job, the model first creates a list of all available, unassigned officers eligible to fill that job. Depending on the way different job characteristics are specified, certain individuals may not appear on that assignment list, perhaps because their grade was too low or because they lacked necessary experience. All officers who meet the prerequisites appear on the assignment list, and that assignment list is sorted according to the desirability of different candidate officers. Officers with characteristics that are *encouraged* will appear higher on this list, while officers with characteristics that are *discouraged* will appear lower on this list.

To obtain information about job characteristics and prerequisites, we used historical personnel data on all core 13S officers to describe the characteristics of officers who filled jobs. To determine the characteristics of individuals who filled specific jobs, we used individual-level FY 2001–2014 personnel data for core 13S officers from the Air Force Personnel Center (AFPC).[6] We validated our findings with the space career field manager. These job characteristics included the following.

- **Grade**: The model discouraged, but did not prohibit, grade substitution.[7] We calculated grade requirements by looking at the distribution of grades attained by officers serving in

---

[5] With infinite computing resources, the user could simply model each position in this set as a separate job in the MCM. Because of computational difficulties and the need to summarize results in a useful manner, we opted to aggregate similar positions into broad job groups.

[6] "Core," when describing an Air Force specialty, designates the primary career field of an individual and is used to distinguish a certain kind of officer, e.g., a space officer (core 13S), from the duty specialty in which the officer currently serves, e.g., a space officer (core 13S) in an instructor position (duty 81T).

[7] To assign officers to jobs, the model first creates a list of available (unassigned) individuals who can possibly fill a particular job and then selects officers to fill that position from the list. Depending on the requirements specified for the job in the model, certain characteristics (such as experience) may prevent officers from appearing on an assignment list because they do not satisfy the requirements. For those who do satisfy requirements, the assignment list is sorted; officers with characteristics that are discouraged will appear lower on the list. If officers do not meet

those positions and choosing the grade range that encompasses the 10th through 90th percentiles. To better understand how IR positions may affect the depth of expertise and seniority in certain areas, we note that in many instances, separate jobs are created for separate grades.

- **Size**: The total number of positions for each job in the model was set in proportion to the number of positions in the FY 2014 MPES data. However, because the model is a steady-state model, the grade distribution of the FY 2014 positions was imbalanced and unsustainable (as discussed above). We rescaled position totals to correspond to what they would be in a steady state, with the proportions of total jobs by grade set to match this distribution.

- **Duration**: For each job, we calculated the distribution of duration for positions aggregated to that job. We used the 10th and 90th percentile of job duration, based on the historical personnel data, to specify the job's minimum and maximum durations. We set the preferred job duration to be equal to the median job duration, calculated over the FY 2001–2014 period.

- **Fill priority**: One of the most important job characteristics in the MCM is the fill priority, which determines the order in which jobs are filled. We initially used the FY 2015 Space Officer Allocation Plan (SOAP) to set the priority for each job. The FY 2015 SOAP describes three broad categories of fill priorities: (1) *must fill*, with a fill rate of 100 percent; (2) *priority fill*, with a fill rate of 90 percent; and (3) *entitlement fill*, which describes positions that are filled to the extent possible, after positions in the other two categories. Based on discussions with the Office of the Director, Space Operations, Deputy Chief of Staff for Operations, Headquarters Air Force (AF/A3S); officers at the Space Operations Force Development and Training, Headquarters Air Force (AF/A3ST); and AFSPC, we expanded the fill priority to four categories to better reflect how jobs within these broad categories are filled in practice. In particular, the priority-fill category, which includes IR jobs, was split into "Priority Fill, High" and "Priority Fill, Low" to distinguish between the prioritization of IR jobs and jobs filled after IR jobs are filled. Table 2.1 shows the list of fill priorities used in the model.

Table 2.1. Fill Priorities

Order	Fill Priorities
One	Must Fill
Two	Priority Fill, High
Three	Priority Fill, Low
Four	Entitlement Fill

NOTE: This table reports the different fill priorities used in the model and the order in which the MCM fills jobs based on those priorities. All jobs are assigned an integer priority with "1" being the highest priority and "4" being the lowest priority, reported in the Order column.

---

the grade requirements for a job, they are still eligible, but they will be ranked below officers who do meet the grade requirements.

- **Repeating jobs**: Repeat assignments were generally allowed, but if over 75 percent of all previous assignments for a particular job did not reflect repeats, then repeats were forbidden. If less than 50 percent of a job's assignments were repeats, then repeats were discouraged.

- **Qualifications**: Certain jobs require previous experiences, and these prerequisites were coded in the model. For example, in certain areas, staff jobs had to be filled by individuals with operational experience in the same areas. As another example, certain senior staff positions had to be filled by individuals who had received adequate development, such as intermediate developmental education (IDE), to the degree reflected in the historical data. We used historical personnel data to validate our choices of experience qualifications in the model. In doing so, we attempt to capture the selectivity of various positions in the 13S career field; positions that are more selective have more intense prerequisites, while those that are less selective have fewer prerequisites.

- **Experience disqualifications and discouragements**: IR experiences take up time in an officer's career. The opportunity cost for an individual officer of filling an IR billet is the loss of time spent doing something else that may be more valuable for career advancement. If an officer has to fill an IR billet, he or she may not complete the necessary prerequisites required for selection in certain top career-field positions. Unfortunately, our ability to determine all of the necessary qualifications and prerequisites for every position from personnel data was limited, particularly for very senior positions, due to small sample sizes. Instead, to model the potential of adverse impact of IR experiences, we directly assumed that IR experiences prevented or discouraged officers from holding other positions. If less than 1 percent of individuals holding a particular job had a particular IR experience (such as accessions, recruiting, or an academic job), we assumed that this IR experience prevented an individual from holding that job. If between 1 and 10 percent of individuals holding a particular job had a particular IR experience, this IR experience was discouraged in the assignment process. However, certain IR positions, such as senior leader support, may actually be desirable for career advancement. If more than 40 percent of individuals holding a particular job had a certain type of IR experience, individuals with this IR experience were encouraged to be assigned to that job. All of this logic was validated with personnel data. Because some positions have small sample sizes, particularly very senior positions, we also cross-checked our decisions with 13S personnel management officers. For details on the extent to which different positions were filled with officers of different types of IR experiences, see the appendix.

- **Retire during job**: If less than 10 percent of individuals did not retire during or immediately after filling a position, retirements after completing the job were forbidden.

In the next subsections, we describe the characteristics of different space jobs in the model and their interrelationships.[8]

---

[8] The full logic of the model is available on request from the authors.

Acquisition Jobs

Space officers serving in acquisition organizations and positions are responsible for the planning, design, and development of space-based surveillance and weapon systems. Space system acquisition is a challenging environment, because systems are expected to survive and work properly for decades, with almost no opportunity for routine maintenance or modification. Because it is difficult to maintain and modify space systems once they have been launched, space systems have unique cost life cycles, with more than 70 percent of total costs in the planning and development phase (Payton, 2009). Space officers serving in acquisition positions will ideally have operational experience and familiarity working with satellite systems and other space-based weapons and surveillance systems, and will need to be able to deal with acquisition challenges unique to space systems.

Table 2.2 reports the basic characteristics of the four different jobs in the acquisition job group. There is one detachment commander (Det/CC) and a mix of acquisition jobs that are broken out by grade. The O-3 acquisition job is encouraged to be filled by an officer with some satellite operations experience, and the O-4/5 and O-6 jobs are preferred to be filled by officers with previous acquisition experience. The Det/CC job is discouraged from being filled by an individual with certain previous IR experiences (academic, recruiting and accessions, and operations IR jobs; see The appendix for more details).

Table 2.2. Acquisition Job Characteristics

Job Description	Job Code	Number of Positions	Grade	Fill Priority
Acquisition, Det/CC	ACQC	1	4,5	Must Fill
Acquisition, O-3	ACQ3	13	3	Entitlement Fill
Acquisition, O-4/5	ACQ4	2	4,5	Entitlement Fill
Acquisition, O-6	ACQ6	1	6	Entitlement Fill
Total		17		

SOURCE: Authors' calculations using MPES, SPECs, and personnel data.

Figure 2.3 presents the total number of positions for acquisition jobs; in the current version of the model, there are only 17 total positions, less than 1 percent of all 13S positions in the model.

Figure 2.3. Acquisition Jobs: Number of Positions

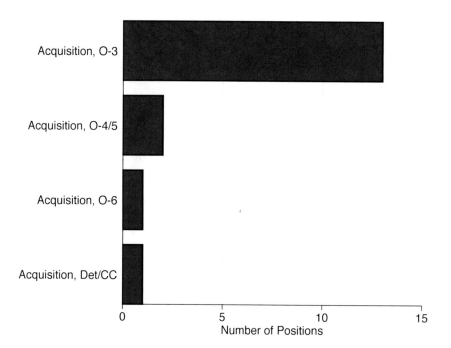

Operations and Staff Jobs

Using the SPEC, we separated operations and staff positions into nine different broad categories:

1. intelligence, surveillance, and reconnaissance (ISR)
2. satellite systems
3. space control
4. space staff
5. space test
6. space warfare
7. spacelift
8. space warning
9. missile defense (staff only).

In general, for the operations positions, most job categories have O-1/2 positions, O-3 positions, O-4+ positions, and Det/CC. Higher grades of jobs prefer (but do not require) the same types of previous operational experience, and higher grades prefer (but do not require) IDE. Individuals with certain types of previous IR experiences are often discouraged from holding Det/CC jobs (see The appendix for details).

Most staff positions are designated by grade and have a hierarchy (wing, numbered Air Force [NAF], major command [MAJCOM], Air Staff, and joint). More staff jobs at the senior levels prefer (but do not require) the same types of previous operational experience, and MAJCOM/Air

11

Staff/joint staff positions prefer (but do not require) IDE. Also, certain IR experiences prevent or discourage officers from holding many senior-level staff positions (see The appendix for details).

Figures 2.4 and 2.5 provide an overview of the operations jobs and staff jobs in the model, showing the total number of positions assigned to each job category.

Figure 2.4. Operations Jobs: Number of Positions

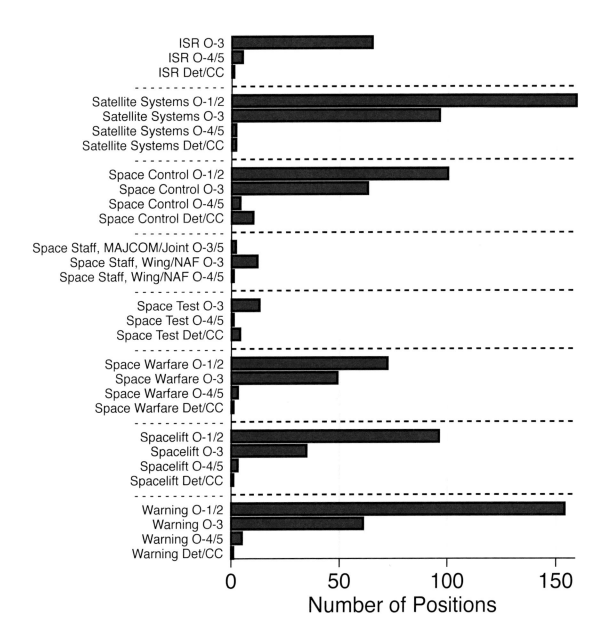

Figure 2.5. Staff Jobs: Number of Positions

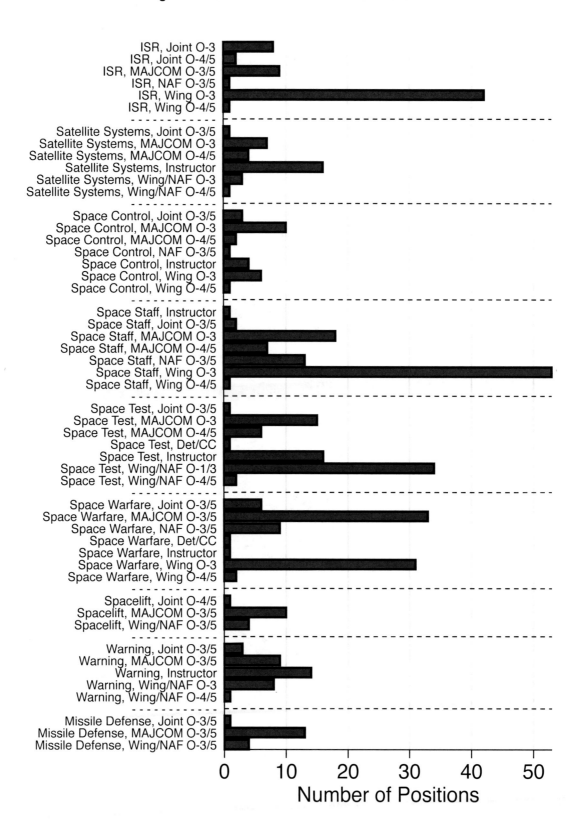

Intelligence, Surveillance, and Reconnaissance

Tables 2.3 and 2.4 report characteristics of ISR operations and staff job groups. Global, integrated ISR operations are conducted throughout the range of military operations; the 13S community conducts ISR using space-based sensors. The primary mission of the 13S ISR community is to use these sensors to enhance and substantiate ISR products, applications, capabilities, and resources for many different users in the military and national security community. Typically, space ISR operators use satellite data, ground-based radar, and other sensors to collect and disseminate information that supports strategic, operational, and tactical decisionmaking (Air Force Doctrine Document 3-14, 2012).

Table 2.3. Operations Job Characteristics: ISR

Job Description	Job Code	Number of Positions	Grade	Fill Priority
ISR Det/CC	OISRC	1	5,6	Must Fill
ISR O-3	OISR3	65	2,3	Must Fill
ISR O-4/5	OISR4	5	4,5	Must Fill
Total		71		

Table 2.4. Staff Job Characteristics: ISR

Job Description	Job Code	Number of Positions	Grade	Fill Priority
ISR, Joint O-3	SISJ3	8	3	Priority Fill, Low
ISR, Joint O-4/5	SISJ4	2	4,5	Priority Fill, Low
ISR, MAJCOM O-3/5	SISM4	9	3,4,5	Priority Fill, Low
ISR, NAF O-3/5	SISN4	1	4,5	Entitlement Fill
ISR, Wing O-3	SISW3	42	3	Priority Fill, Low
ISR, Wing O-4/5	SISW4	1	4,5,6	Priority Fill, Low
Total		63		

Examples of units active in ISR operations include the 6th Satellite Operations Squadron (SOPS), which manages the Defense Meteorological Satellite Program and Defense Weather Satellite System. This unit captures and delivers some of the most timely and accurate environmental intelligence data in the world. The Space-Based Radar program, administered by AFSPC's Space and Missile Systems Center and the National Reconnaissance Office, uses satellite assets to conduct continuous multitheater surveillance, identification, tracking, and targeting of ground-moving targets in support of combat operations.

The ISR operations job categories include one detachment commander position, 65 positions for O-3s, and five positions for O4s/O5s. There were 63 different staff ISR positions, most of which were medium priority.

Satellite Systems

Satellite communications allow governments and individuals to communicate accurately across the globe. Satellite systems, which enable satellite communications, provide a broad range of capabilities, including instant access to the global information grid, secure transmission of critical intelligence, and situational awareness for operations conducted in remote environments that lack communications infrastructure.

In the 13S career field, satellite operators maneuver and direct space-based satellite assets that provide information on global positioning, navigation, and timing, using a variety of different satellites. These satellites provide services beyond the realm of national security and govern many different economic activities, including transportation, critical to our economic infrastructure (Air Force Doctrine Document 3-14, 2012).

Units active in satellite systems operations include 1 SOPS, at Schreiver Air Force Base, Colorado, which commands, controls, and operates the Space Based Space Surveillance system, the Advanced Technology Risk Reduction system, and the Geosynchronous Space Situational Awareness Program. 2 SOPS, also at Schreiver Air Force Base, performs the satellite command and control (C2) mission for the Global Positioning System.

Tables 2.5 and 2.6 report characteristics of the jobs in satellite systems operations and staff groups. This category represents a mix of grades in a large category of operations jobs, with approximately 15.2 percent of the total 13S positions. These jobs are among the highest-priority jobs in the 13S career field. Staff positions, many of which are lower priority, include instructor positions, joint and MAJCOM staff positions, and a handful of wing/NAF-level staff positions.

Table 2.5. Operations Job Characteristics: Satellite Systems

Job Description	Job Code	Number of Positions	Grade	Fill Priority
Satellite Systems Det/CC	OSATC	2	4,5	Must Fill
Satellite Systems O-1/2	OSAT1	159	1,2	Must Fill
Satellite Systems O-3	OSAT3	96	3	Must Fill
Satellite Systems O-4/5	OSAT4	2	4,5	Must Fill
Total		259		

Table 2.6. Staff Job Characteristics: Satellite Systems

Job Description	Job Code	Number of Positions	Grade	Fill Priority
Satellite Systems, Instructor	SSATT	16	2,3,4	Must Fill
Satellite Systems, Joint O-3/5	SSAJ4	1	4,5,6	Priority Fill, Low
Satellite Systems, MAJCOM O-3	SSAM3	7	3	Priority Fill, Low
Satellite Systems, MAJCOM O-4/5	SSAM4	4	4,5	Priority Fill, Low
Satellite Systems, Wing/NAF O-3	SSAW3	3	2,3	Entitlement Fill
Satellite Systems, Wing/NAF O-4/5	SSAW4	1	4,5,6	Entitlement Fill
Total		32		

Space Control

In the 13S career field, space control operations are executed to protect U.S. military and allied space capabilities while denying space capabilities to adversaries. Space control operations, which can be offensive or defensive, include protective and defensive measures to ensure that friendly forces can continuously conduct space operations across the entire spectrum of conflict, and operations to deceive, disrupt, or destroy adversarial space capabilities (Air Force Doctrine Document 3-14, 2012).

Table 2.7 and 2.8 report characteristics of the jobs in space control operations and staff groups. With 177 positions, or approximately 10.4 percent of the total 13S positions, space control operations are a large and important mission area for the 13S career field. These jobs are all very high priority.

Table 2.7. Operations Job Characteristics: Space Control

Job Description	Job Code	Number of Positions	Grade	Fill Priority
Space Control Det/CC	OCONC	10	3,4,5,6	Must Fill
Space Control O-1/2	OCON1	100	1,2	Must Fill
Space Control O-3	OCON3	63	3	Must Fill
Space Control O-4/5	OCON4	4	4,5	Must Fill
Total		177		

16

Table 2.8. Staff Job Characteristics: Space Control

Job Description	Job Code	Number of Positions	Grade	Fill Priority
Space Control, Instructor	SCONT	4	3,4	Must Fill
Space Control, Joint O-3/5	SCOJ4	3	3,4,5,6	Priority Fill, Low
Space Control, MAJCOM O-3	SCOM3	10	3	Priority Fill, Low
Space Control, MAJCOM O-4/5	SCOM4	2	4,5,6	Priority Fill, Low
Space Control, NAF O-3/5	SCON4	1	3,4,5,6	Priority Fill, Low
Space Control, Wing O-3	SCOW3	6	3	Priority Fill, High
Space Control, Wing O-4/5	SCOW4	1	4,5,6	Priority Fill, High
Total		27		

Space Staff

Tables 2.9 and 2.10 report characteristics of the jobs in the space staff group, focusing on operations and staff jobs, respectively.[9] Operations staff jobs include a handful of executive officer positions, positions in commander's action groups, and MAJCOM or joint-level staff positions. These positions are not as highly prioritized as some of the other operations positions. Nonoperations space staff represent a fairly large category of positions, though many have relatively lower fill priority.

Table 2.9. Operations Job Characteristics: Space Staff

Job Description	Job Code	Number of Positions	Grade	Fill Priority
Ops, Space Staff, MAJCOM/Joint O-3/5	OSTFJ	2	3,4,5	Priority Fill, Low
Ops, Space Staff, Wing/NAF O-3	OSTW3	12	2,3	Entitlement Fill
Ops, Space Staff, Wing/NAF O-4/5	OSTW4	1	4,5,6	Entitlement Fill
Total		15		

---

[9] The SPEC is a hierarchical system for classifying positions; an interesting feature of this system is that space staff can be found within both the operations and staff categories. Because we use the SPEC in creating job categories for the model, we follow this in our model.

Table 2.10. Staff Job Characteristics: Space Staff

Job Description	Job Code	Number of Positions	Grade	Fill Priority
Staff, Space Staff, Instructor	SSTFT	1	3,4,5	Priority Fill, Low
Staff, Space Staff, Joint O-3/5	SSTJ4	2	4,5,6	Priority Fill, Low
Staff, Space Staff, MAJCOM O-3	SSTM3	18	3	Priority Fill, Low
Staff, Space Staff, MAJCOM O-4/5	SSTM4	7	4,5,6	Priority Fill, Low
Staff, Space Staff, NAF O-3/5	SSTN4	13	3,4,5	Entitlement Fill
Staff, Space Staff, Wing O-3	SSTW3	53	3	Priority Fill, Low
Staff, Space Staff, Wing O-4/5	SSTW4	1	4,5	Priority Fill, Low
Total		95		

Space Test

As part of the space career field's space support operations, space test operational units provide testing and evaluation of existing and new satellite systems. Tables 2.11 and 2.12 report characteristics of the jobs in the space test group, focusing on operations and staff jobs, respectively. Although most 13S space test–related positions are staff positions, operations positions represent the 18 nonmissile space test positions at the Air Force Technical Applications Center. Staff positions in the space test category encompass a large category of positions and include one detachment commander position, 16 instructor positions, one joint staff position, and many different wing/NAF and MAJCOM-level staff positions.

Table 2.11. Operations Job Characteristics: Space Test

Job Description	Job Code	Number of Positions	Grade	Fill Priority
Space Test Det/CC	OTSTC	4	3,4,5	Must Fill
Space Test O-3	OTST3	13	3	Priority Fill, Low
Space Test O-4/5	OTST4	1	4,5	Priority Fill, Low
Total		18		

Table 2.12. Staff Job Characteristics: Space Test

Job Description	Job Code	Number of Positions	Grade	Fill Priority
Space Test, Det/CC	STSTC	1	4,5,6	Must Fill
Space Test, Instructor	STSTT	16	3,4	Priority Fill, Low
Space Test, Joint O-3/5	STSJ4	1	3,4,5	Priority Fill, Low
Space Test, MAJCOM O-3	STSM3	15	3	Priority Fill, Low
Space Test, MAJCOM O-4/5	STSM4	6	4,5	Priority Fill, Low
Space Test, Wing/NAF O-1/3	STSW3	34	3	Entitlement Fill
Space Test, Wing/NAF O-4/5	STSW4	2	4,5	Entitlement Fill
Total		75		

Space Warfare Command and Control Operations

Tables 2.13 and 2.14 report characteristics of the operations and staff jobs in the space warfare C2 group. These positions include certain legacy positions (such as those at the now restructured Space Innovation and Development Center, formerly the Space Warfare Center), but they also include other positions in space area of concern (AOC) units (e.g., 14 Air Force, 614 SOPS, Headquarters Air Force Space Command Center, 9 SOPS Vandenberg, 21 Wing Operations Center), theater AOC units (e.g., 603 AOC Ramstein, 32 Air Operations Squadron Ramstein, 608 Combat Operations Squadron Barksdale, 612 Combat Plans Squadron, Davis Monthan, 9 Information Warfare Flight Shaw, 609 Combat Operations Squadron Shaw, 56 Air Operations Squadron Hickam) and others.

Table 2.13. Operations Job Characteristics: Space Warfare C2

Job Description	Job Code	Number of Positions	Grade	Fill Priority
Space Warfare C2 Det/CC	OWARC	1	4,5,6	Must Fill
Space Warfare C2 O-1/2	OWAR1	72	1,2	Entitlement Fill
Space Warfare C2 O-3	OWAR3	49	3	Entitlement Fill
Space Warfare C2 O-4/5	OWAR4	3	4,5	Entitlement Fill
Total		125		

Table 2.14. Staff Job Characteristics: Space Warfare C2

Job Description	Job Code	Number of Positions	Grade	Fill Priority
Space Warfare C2, Det/CC	SWARC	1	4,5	Must Fill
Space Warfare C2, Instructor	SWART	1	3,4	Must Fill
Space Warfare C2, Joint O-3/5	SWAJ4	6	3,4,5	Entitlement Fill
Space Warfare C2, MAJCOM O-3/5	SWAM4	33	3,4,5	Entitlement Fill
Space Warfare C2, NAF O-3/5	SWAN4	9	3,4,5	Entitlement Fill
Space Warfare C2, Wing O-3	SWAW3	31	3	Entitlement Fill
Space Warfare C2, Wing O-4/5	SWAW4	2	4,5	Entitlement Fill
Total		83		

Spacelift

Spacelift operations are responsible for physically delivering satellites, payloads, and other material into space. These operations are conducted to deploy, enhance, or sustain space-based capabilities that enhance satellite communications, intelligence gathering, positioning, navigation, and other national security objectives. Spacelift operations begin by generating a launch campaign, which prepares launch vehicles and facilities for launch. Performing the launch and successfully completing the spacelift mission process constitutes the end of the mission campaign (Air Force Doctrine Document 3-14, 2012).

Tables 2.15 and 2.16 reports characteristics of the jobs in the spacelift operations and staff groups. The 135 operations jobs, separated by grade and detachment commander, are all very high fill priority. There are fewer staff positions in spacelift, and they tend to have a much lower fill priority than the operations positions.

Table 2.15. Operations Job Characteristics: Spacelift

Job Description	Job Code	Number of Positions	Grade	Fill Priority
Spacelift Det/CC	OLFTC	1	4,5	Must Fill
Spacelift O-1/2	OLFT1	96	1,2	Must Fill
Spacelift O-3	OLFT3	35	3	Must Fill
Spacelift O-4/5	OLFT4	3	4,5	Must Fill
Total		135		

Table 2.16. Staff Job Characteristics: Spacelift

Job Description	Job Code	Number of Positions	Grade	Fill Priority
Spacelift, Joint O-4/5	SLFJ4	1	4,5,6	Priority Fill, Low
Spacelift, MAJCOM O-3/5	SLFM4	10	3,4,5	Must Fill
Spacelift, Wing/NAF O-3/5	SLFW4	4	3,4,5	Must Fill
Total		15		

Space Warning

Space warning jobs involve a variety of different intelligence functions to detect and report time-sensitive information on foreign developments that could indicate a threat. Launch detection, which uses space and ground-based sensors, provides real-time information on foreign space launches. Missile tracking operations support missile warning and missile defense systems using a mix of space- and ground-based sensors (Air Force Doctrine Document 3-14, 2012).

Tables 2.17 and 2.18 report characteristics of the jobs in the space warning operations and staff groups. The 221 operations jobs, separated by grade and detachment commander, are also all high fill priority, while the much smaller number of staff jobs tend to be lower fill priority.

Table 2.17. Operations Job Characteristics: Space Warning

Job Description	Job Code	Number of Positions	Grade	Fill Priority
Space Warning Det/CC	OWRNC	1	5	Must Fill
Space Warning O-1/2	OWRN1	154	1,2	Must Fill
Space Warning O-3	OWRN3	61	3	Must Fill
Space Warning O-4/5	OWRN4	5	4,5	Must Fill
Total		221		

Table 2.18. Staff Job Characteristics: Space Warning

Job Description	Job Code	Number of Positions	Grade	Fill Priority
Space Warning, Instructor	SWRNT	14	2,3,4	Must Fill
Space Warning, Joint O-3/5	SWRJ4	3	3,4,5	Priority Fill, Low
Space Warning, MAJCOM O-3/5	SWRM4	9	3,4,5	Priority Fill, Low
Space Warning, Wing/NAF O-3	SWRW3	8	3	Entitlement Fill
Space Warning, Wing/NAF O-4/5	SWRW4	1	4,5	Entitlement Fill
Total		35		

Missile Defense Staff Jobs

A final category, only relevant for staff jobs, consists of several different missile defense jobs. These tend to be legacy positions that are, to a certain extent, the responsibility of the nuclear (13N) career field, but are still 13S billets as of FY 2014. There are no operational positions in this job group. Table 2.19 reports characteristics of the positions in the missile defense staff group. This category amounts to a relatively small number of positions (18), most of which are low fill priority, although some (the joint staff positions) are very high profile.

Table 2.19. Staff Job Characteristics: Missile Defense

Job Description	Job Code	Number of Positions	Grade	Fill Priority
Missile Defense, Joint O-3/5	SMIJ4	1	4,5,6	Priority Fill, Low
Missile Defense, MAJCOM O-3/5	SMIM4	13	3,4,5	Priority Fill, Low
Missile Defense, Wing/NAF O-3/5	SMIW4	4	3,4,5	Entitlement Fill
Total		18		

IR Job Group

No IR positions are coded explicitly for space officers. Rather, the Air Force taxes career fields to fill these positions. Consequently, at any time, some portion of the 13S officer population is filling IR positions, rather than 13S positions. To account for these in the MCM, we created an IR job group containing IR jobs. As described in the previous chapter, we grouped

IR positions into the job groups listed in Table 1.1. We reviewed historical personnel data to see how many 13S officers were serving in IR jobs on average and included these jobs in the MCM. The 12 IR jobs used in the model are listed in Table 2.20. These jobs include that are anecdotally considered by many officers to be "career enhancing," such as functional command (four total positions) and senior leader support (43 total positions). They also include positions that are sometimes considered to not be career enhancing, like academic IRs (56 total positions), operations IRs (65 total positions), and recruiting (46 total positions). All IR positions are broken out by grade and are given a "priority-fill, high" rating, after must-fill positions, based on the priority stated in the SOAP. The relative sizes of the IR categories are depicted in Figure 2.6.

There are two major ways that IR jobs affect the fill rates of other positions. First, IR jobs have a relatively high fill priority; they must be filled before some other career field positions, taking labor away from lower-priority space jobs. Second, discussions with career field managers; stakeholders in Deputy Chief of Staff, Manpower, Personnel, and Services (AF/A1); and assignment officers at AFPC reveal a widespread belief that serving in certain IRs, such as academics or recruiting, can negatively impact officers' careers and reduce their later opportunities to serve in senior-level staff positions or as detachment commanders. To attempt to measure the extent to which this occurs in practice, we calculated the instances in which these desired positions were filled by officers with IR experience. As discussed previously, if less than 1 percent of individuals who historically filled a position had a particular IR experience, we forbade officers from taking that position. If between 1 and 10 percent of officers who filled a position had a particular IR experience, the model discouraged officers from taking that position.[10]

Intuitively, we would expect to find that reducing IRs, particularly jobs in the less–career enhancing categories, increases fill rates for lower-priority space positions. We would also expect that reducing IRs would increase fill rates for positions that had discouraged particular IR experiences. We investigate these hypotheses in the next chapter.

---

[10] The appendix provides statistics on the total employment periods for each job and whether they were filled by officers with different types of IR experiences.

Table 2.20. IR Job Characteristics

Description	Code	Number of Positions	Grade	Fill Priority
IR Functional Command	IRFUN	4	5,6	Priority Fill, High
IR Senior Leader Support, O-3	IRLE3	4	3	Priority Fill, High
IR Senior Leader Support, O-4/5	IRLE4	39	4,5,6	Priority Fill, High
IR Academic, O-3	IRAC3	15	2,3	Priority Fill, High
IR Academic, O-4/5	IRAC4	41	4,5	Priority Fill, High
IR Operations, O-3	IROP3	3	3	Priority Fill, High
IR Operations, O-4/5	IROP4	40	4,5	Priority Fill, High
IR Operations, O-6	IROP6	22	6	Priority Fill, High
IR Recruiting, O-3	IRRE3	9	2,3	Priority Fill, High
IR Recruiting, O-4/5	IRRE4	31	4,5	Priority Fill, High
IR Recruiting, O-6	IRRE6	6	6	Priority Fill, High
Total		214		

Figure 2.6. IR Jobs: Number of Positions

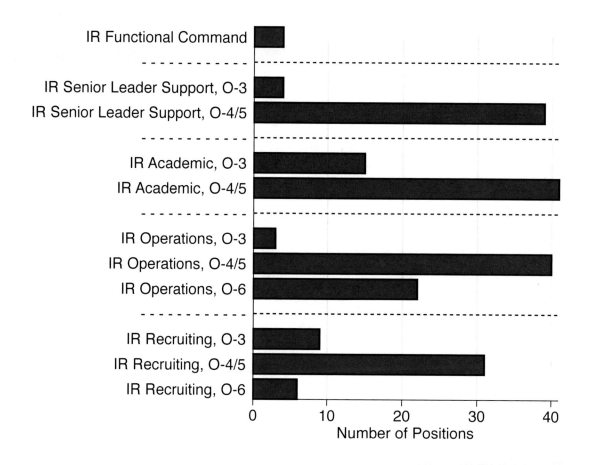

23

Education and Development Job Group

In addition to the operational, staff, acquisition, and IR jobs in the model, we include two "jobs" for long-term education and development. Continuing education is very important for a technical field like space, and officers use continuing education to maintain and acquire skills in a variety of different areas, including contracts, systems engineering, system design, simulation, or artificial intelligence (Beary et al., 2007). A review of the historical data indicates that several space jobs have an experience at Air Force Institute of Technology (AFIT) or a developmental education tour as a prerequisite. Including a job group for assignments to education and development opportunities allows for the MDM to account for officers who are pursuing advanced academic degrees at AFIT as well as those participating in IDE and senior developmental education. The characteristics of these "jobs" appear in Table 2.21.

Table 2.21. Education and Development Job Characteristics

Description	Code	Number of Positions	Grade	Fill Priority
Intermediate Developmental Education	TRIDE	30	4	Entitlement Fill
Senior Developmental Education	TRSDE	25	5,6	Entitlement Fill
Total		55		

Summary

Table 2.22 reports a summary of the total number of authorizations and positions by grade, both for the FY 2014 inventory and the steady-state model. Our model maintains the total number of space officer inventory and positions for FY 2014, but it redistributes the positions and authorizations according to the steady-state grade distribution, depicted in Figure 2.1. Note that we kept the grade distribution for the IR and education positions the same as in FY 2014, in order to determine what effect reducing those positions would have on steady-state fill rates and inventory.

In the next chapter, we summarize findings from running the model under a variety of IR scenarios.

Table 2.22. Summary of Authorizations and Positions, FY 2014 and Steady State

Grade	FY 2014			MCM		
	Authorizations	13S Positions	IR and Education Positions	Authorizations	13S Positions	IR and Education Positions
O-1	256	231	0	315	284	0
O-2	150	135	7	305	274	7
O-3	536	483	24	806	726	24
O-4	358	322	126	167	151	126
O-5	330	297	67	76	68	67
O-6	59	53	45	20	18	45
O-7	1	1	0	1	1	0
Total 13S	**1,690**	**1,522**	**269**	**1,690**	**1,522**	**269**

3. Results: Reducing the Number of IR Positions

As part of our research, we conducted several policy experiments that involve reducing the number of IR positions in the model. In particular, we focused on reducing the number of accessions, recruiting, academic, and operations IRs, which are thought to be less desirable and represent a loss of labor for the career field. We maintain the current number of command and senior leader support (aide-de-camp and executive officers) IRs in this analysis, because these are desirable positions that are considered beneficial to officers' careers.

We first describe results for the baseline run of the model. For this baseline, we calibrated the model as described in Chapter Two and used it to study how the career field would evolve if accessions, promotion policies, and retention rates were kept at their FY 2014 levels for many years. Next, we reduce the number of IR jobs assigned to the 13S career field and summarize the effect on the fill rates of different types of positions. Finally, we explore one simulation, a 50-percent reduction in the number of IR positions, in greater detail.

Baseline Results

In this section, we report the results of the baseline model. We first describe the overall end-strength patterns and average grade distribution of simulated officers. Next, we describe the relationship between the model's implied retention patterns and those we observe in the actual personnel data. Finally, we describe baseline fill rate information for the jobs in the model.

End Strength and Grade Distribution

Figure 3.1 represents the end strength of the model against simulation time. Each bar in the figure depicts the total number of officers by grade that appeared in the 13S career field in each period. It is easy to see that in early periods, the model has relatively fewer senior-grade officers because they have to be promoted from previous grades over time. However, at some point, the total number of officers in each grade is more stable. The horizontal red line at the top of this graph plots the FY 2014 end-strength total of 1,690 officers, approximately what the model delivers in terms of a steady-state inventory level (based on the accession levels and retention profile discussed in Chapter Two).

Figure 3.1. Grade Distribution of 13S Officers in Baseline Model

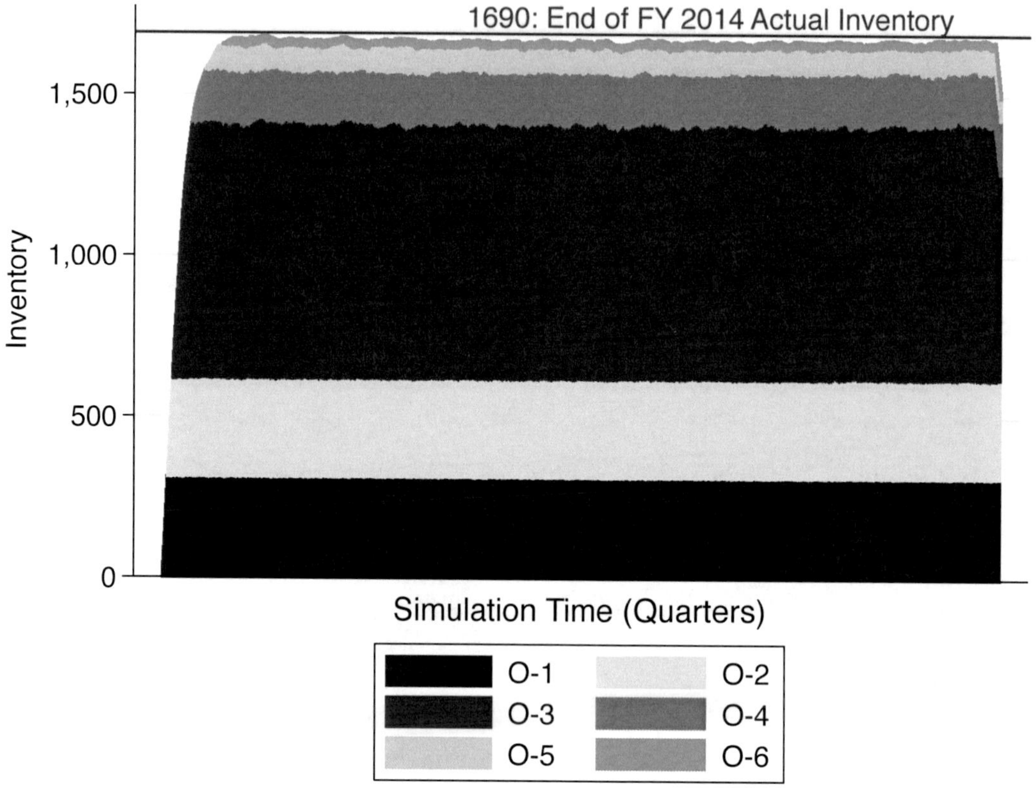

Retention

Figure 3.2 reports the model's retention probabilities (in blue) plotted against the historical retention probabilities from Figure 2.6 (in red). As expected, the model's retention probabilities fit those supplied by AF/A1PF quite well, though not perfectly. One major reason for the difference in retention probabilities is that the actual probabilities only change annually (and are shown to be constant within years), while the model runs quarterly, with retention probabilities changing throughout the year. Naturally, we would expect the model's implied probabilities to change more gradually than the actual data.

Figure 3.2. Retention Probability by Commissioned Years of Service (Baseline Model and Actual)

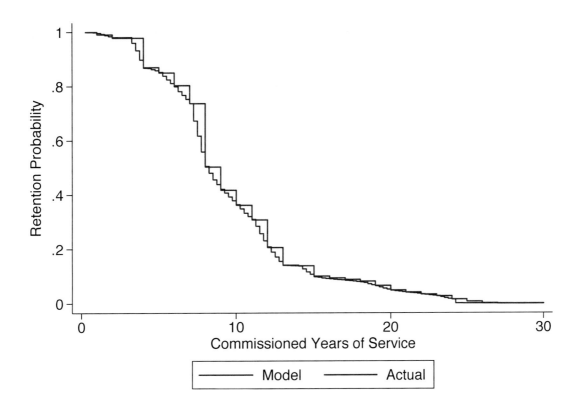

SOURCE: AF/A1PF and authors' calculations.

Average Fill Rates of Jobs

Next, we explore the extent to which the baseline personnel policies, if continued, would allow the filling of 13S officer jobs. Overall, the model yielded a 96-percent manning rate for acquisitions, staff, and operations positions, where this percentage is calculated as an average over the 300-year period for which the model is simulated.[11] In Figure 3.3, we plot the average total number of filled and unfilled positions for 13S acquisition jobs. In this figure, blue bars represent filled positions and white bars represent unfilled positions. Although there are only a small number of acquisition jobs, in the baseline model, three of the 17 positions went unfilled. These positions were at the O-4/5 and O-6 levels. These positions were "entitlement-fill" priority, and there are a relatively small number of senior officers in the steady-state model, which explains why these positions are more likely to be unfilled than others.

---

[11] We allow approximately 40 years for the model to "burn in," so that it reflects a steady-state inventory level and results are not a function of the model being brought up to speed.

Figure 3.3. Filled and Unfilled Positions: Acquisition Jobs

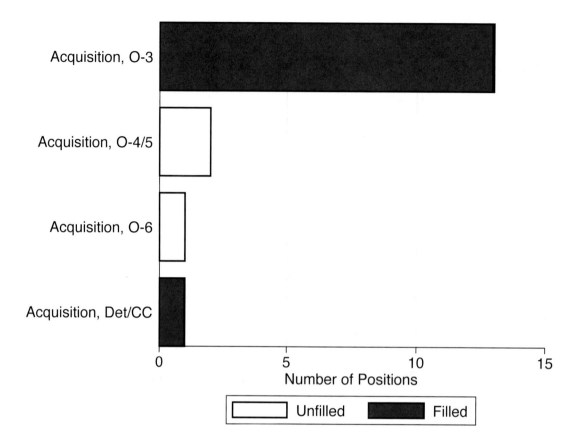

Figure 3.4 plots the average total number of filled and unfilled positions for 13S operations jobs. In general, most operations jobs were filled, with an overall 97.6-percent average fill rate. Low-priority jobs tended to have the lower fill rates, particularly those in the space warfare C2 category.

Figure 3.4. Filled and Unfilled Positions: Operations Jobs

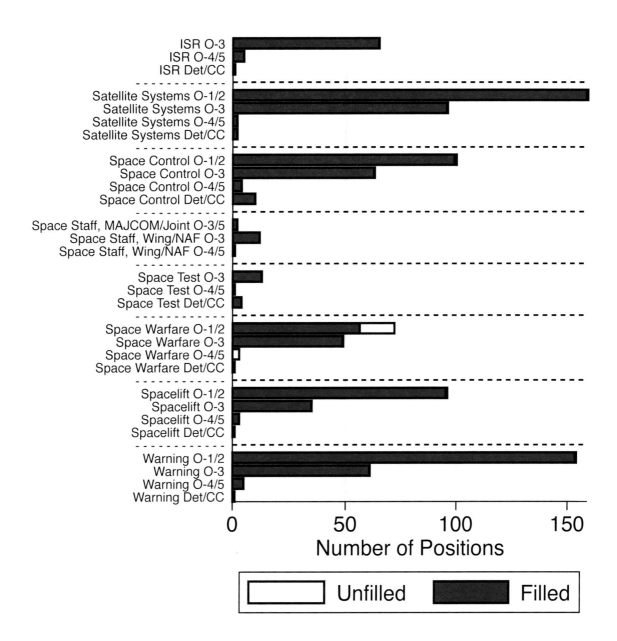

Figure 3.5 plots the average total number of filled and unfilled positions for operations jobs. Of the four different job categories, staff jobs had the most number of unfilled positions in the baseline model, with an average fill rate of just over 92.8 percent. Some positions—particularly the space staff, MAJCOM-level O-4/5 position and the space warfare, wing O-4/5 position—had exceptionally low fill rates.

Figure 3.5. Filled and Unfilled Positions: Staff Positions

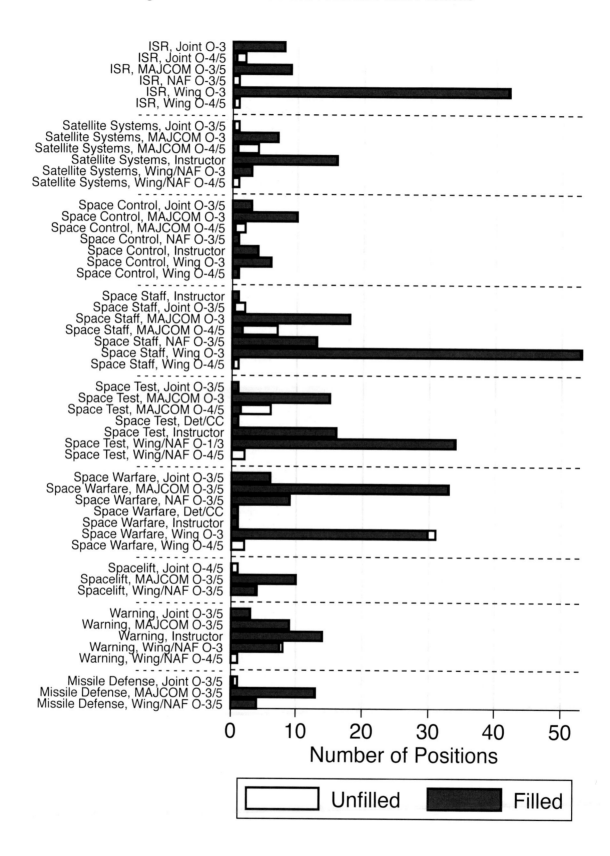

Figure 3.6 shows the average total number of filled and unfilled positions for IR jobs. Because the IR jobs are set to a relatively high priority, the model tries to fill these jobs before it fills many others. IR jobs tend to be filled by individuals in more senior grades (O-3 and above), and that having certain types of IR experience may discourage or prevent an officer from filling other positions later in his or her career.

Figure 3.6. Filled and Unfilled Positions: IR Jobs

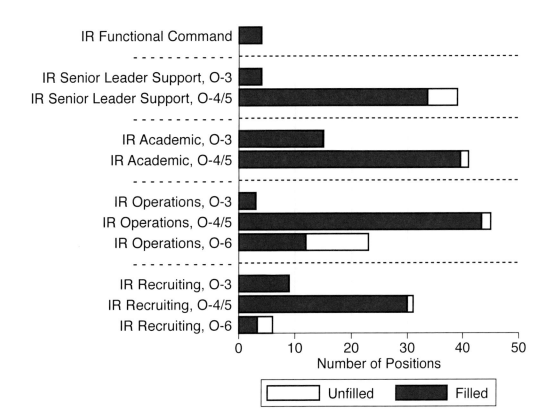

Changing IRs: Results Overview

To evaluate the impact of IRs on personnel outcomes for the 13S career field, we conducted simulations that varied the total number of IR positions that needed to be filled with space officers. In doing this, we focused on reducing only the less–career enhancing IR positions, namely those from the academic, operations, and recruiting categories (see Table 2.19). Here, we provide a brief overview for how the simulated changes to the number of IR positions affected aggregate personnel outcomes, focusing on average fill rates for career field positions. In the next subsection, we investigate model results in more detail.

In Figure 3.7, we present the average fill rate of staff positions on the *y*-axis against the percentage change in IR jobs on the *x*-axis. Each dot on the graph is produced from a separate simulation, where we changed the number of positions of each IR job to a different percentage of the actual total. The vertical dashed line indicates the baseline scenario, where we kept the number of IR positions set to 100 percent of their FY 2014 total. To the left of this vertical line, we reduce the number of IR positions from 95 to 5 percent of this total, and to the right, we increase the number of IR positions from 105 to 195 percent of the total.

The figure shows a negative relationship between the number of IR positions and the average total fill rates of staff jobs. As we increase the number of IR positions, the average fill rate of staff positions decreases, from a baseline of 92.8 percent to approximately 88.7 percent when IR jobs are nearly doubled. Similarly, as we reduce the number of IR positions, the average fill rate for staff positions increases.

Figure 3.7. Average Fill Rates of Staff Positions vs. IR Jobs

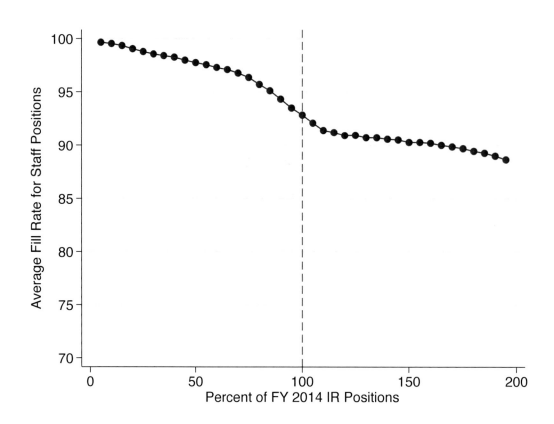

SOURCE: Authors' calculations. Each dot on this graph represents the aggregate results from a separate simulation.

Figure 3.8 presents a similar plot, except now we focus on the relationship between IR positions and the average fill rate of space operations jobs. Because many operations jobs are higher priority than staff and IR positions, reducing IRs has substantially less of an effect on the average fill rate of operations positions, resulting in a much flatter response line. This suggests that IRs are not as much of a concern when it comes to filling operations positions because operations positions tend to be higher fill priority than IR positions—therefore, they do not compete with IR positions for labor.

Figure 3.8. Fill Rates of Operations Positions vs. IR Jobs

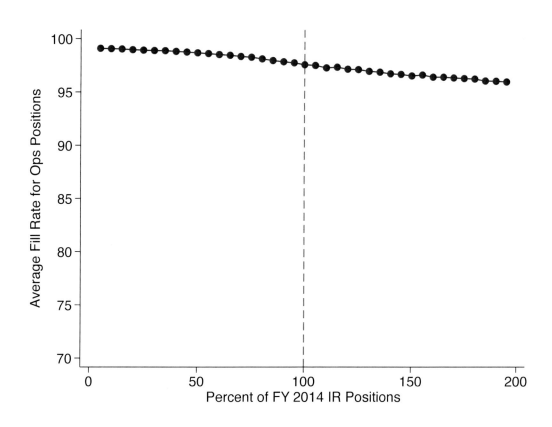

SOURCE: Authors' calculations. Each dot on this graph represents the aggregate results from a separate simulation.

34

Figure 3.9 presents the same plot for space acquisition jobs. Here, the average fill rate stays around 82 percent, until IR jobs are reduced by more than 60 percent. This is because most of the unfilled acquisitions positions are very low priority; only after IR jobs are substantially reduced would officers be available to fill these positions.

Figure 3.9. Fill Rates of Acquisition Positions vs. IR Jobs

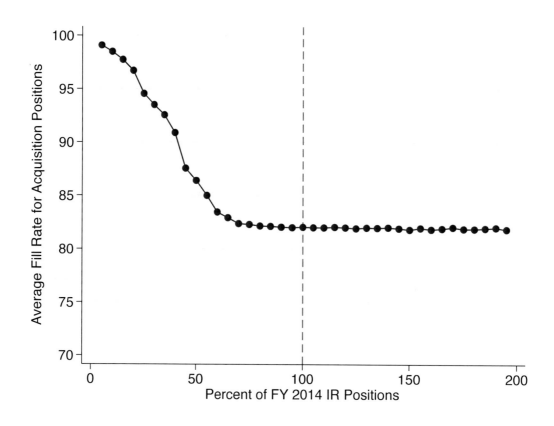

SOURCE: Authors' calculations. Each dot on this graph represents the aggregate results from a separate simulation.

Figure 3.10 plots the relationship between average fill rates and IR jobs for staff, operations, and acquisition jobs separated into fill priority categories: must fill (in blue), priority fill (in green), and entitlement fill (in red).[12] As expected, must-fill jobs are almost always filled, so reducing IRs does not have any impact on their average fill rates, and the response lines tend to be very flat. Interestingly, for staff jobs, increasing the number of IR positions may slightly reduce the average fill rate of high-priority staff jobs. This could be because a large number of IR positions draw labor away from positions that serve as prerequisites for senior-level, must-fill positions. However, this effect seems to be very small and only apply to staff positions.

---

[12] Note that we only report three priority categories in Figure 3.10, aggregating the "priority-fill, high" and "priority-fill, low" categories into the green line.

Figure 3.10. Fill Rates vs. IR Jobs by Priority

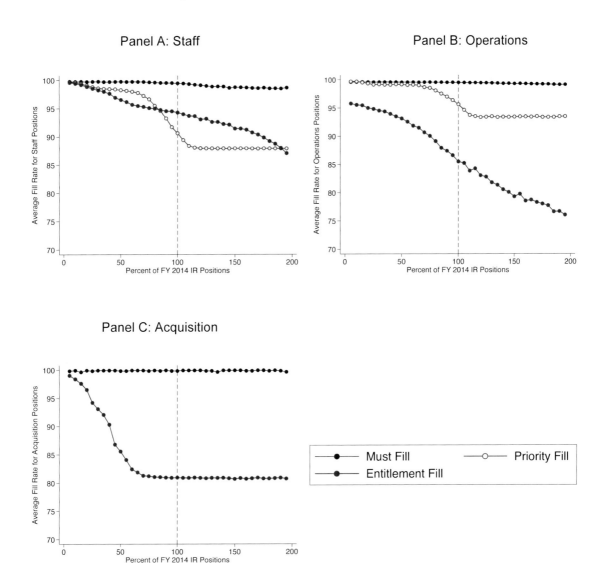

SOURCE: Authors' calculations. Each dot on this graph represents the aggregate results from a separate simulation. The priority-fill category combines jobs in the priority-fill, high and priority-fill, low categories. There are no priority-fill positions in the Acquisition job category.

Priority-fill jobs, which are mostly prioritized just below IRs (although some are at the same level), show a significant negative relationship between their average fill rates and the number of IR positions. However, the negative effect tends to taper off as IR positions are increased substantially. The average fill rates of entitlement-fill jobs respond to changes in IRs even more dramatically than the priority-fill jobs. Entitlement-fill positions represent slack in the system, and when greater constraints are placed upon the system, such as an increase in the number of IR jobs that have to be filled, the fill rates of these entitlement positions will often be the first to respond.

36

Finally, in Figure 3.11, we examine how changing the number of IR positions changes the average fill rates of different positions by grade. In general, the biggest responses occur for O-4 staff positions; most other categories do not show any substantial response, except O-5 positions in acquisition, which show a significant change after the number of IR positions is drastically decreased. Because many IR positions require at least an O-4 grade, this is exactly what we would expect to find.

Figure 3.11. Fill Rates vs. IR Jobs by Grade

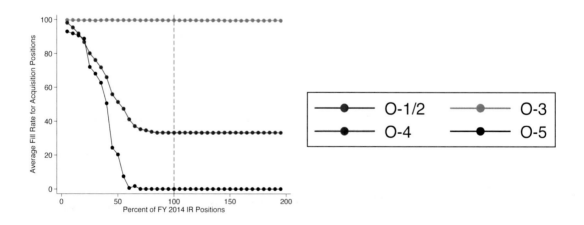

SOURCE: Authors' calculations. Each dot on this graph represents the aggregate results from a separate simulation.

In summary, the MCM simulations suggest that IR jobs attract labor away from certain staff, operations, and acquisitions positions and prevent those jobs from being filled. The effects are the largest on staff positions, particularly relatively low-priority positions that are manned by

O-4s, because many of these positions compete directly with labor that would otherwise be sent to IR jobs. Such positions are lower-priority fills than IR jobs, and these jobs tend to be available only to higher-grade officers.

In meetings across the space officer career field, stakeholders stated that reducing the number of IR positions that space officers needed to fill would produce significant improvements in manning—but our model results do not support this hypothesis. MCM simulations suggest that reducing 95 percent of the academic, accessions, recruiting, and operations IR jobs results in a manning rate of approximately 99.6 percent. This is an increase over the current modeled 96-percent manning rate, but the steady-state manning rate was already quite high to begin with.

Detailed Results: IR Reduction of 50 Percent

Next, we explore more-detailed results from a comparison of outcomes in the baseline scenario to those from the scenario where we cut the total number of academic, operations, and recruiting IR positions in half. This amounts to a reduction of IR positions from a baseline of 214 to 107 positions. This scenario corresponds to the 50-percent dot in Figures 3.8–3.11. Under this scenario, the overall manning rate calculated across all positions increased from 96 percent to 98.3 percent.

Changes in Fill Rates of Different Types of Jobs

In Figure 3.12, we present the average change in fill rates for staff, operations, and acquisition positions, plotting the average difference in the number of filled positions between the 50-percent IR reduction and the baseline scenario. Blue bars denote increases in the number of filled positions, while red bars denote reductions. In general, the figure shows that while cutting IR jobs tends to increase the fill rates of many staff positions, some positions benefit more than others. For instance, for several MAJCOM-level O-4/5 staff jobs (Panel A), between four to five additional positions were filled, on average, as IR jobs are reduced, while other staff positions benefit far less. Note that while many positions have red bars, indicating that the number of average filled positions have fallen, these changes are extremely small, often amounting to less than one-tenth of a position. These negligible decreases, which are probably produced by randomness in the simulations, are not worth serious consideration.

Generally, the jobs that benefit the most tend to be jobs that are O-4/5–level positions that are assigned the "entitlement-fill" priority. The results shown in the figure also confirm that very high-priority jobs are typically unaffected by reducing IRs. Note that in the operations positions (Panel B), the large increase in the fill rates of space warfare O-1/2 is actually produced by an increase in above-grade fills. Some O-3s who were previously filling IR positions are now sent to fill the space warfare O-1/2 positions.

Figure 3.12. Average Change in Fills of Staff Positions: Baseline vs. 50-Percent IR Reduction

Panel A: Staff

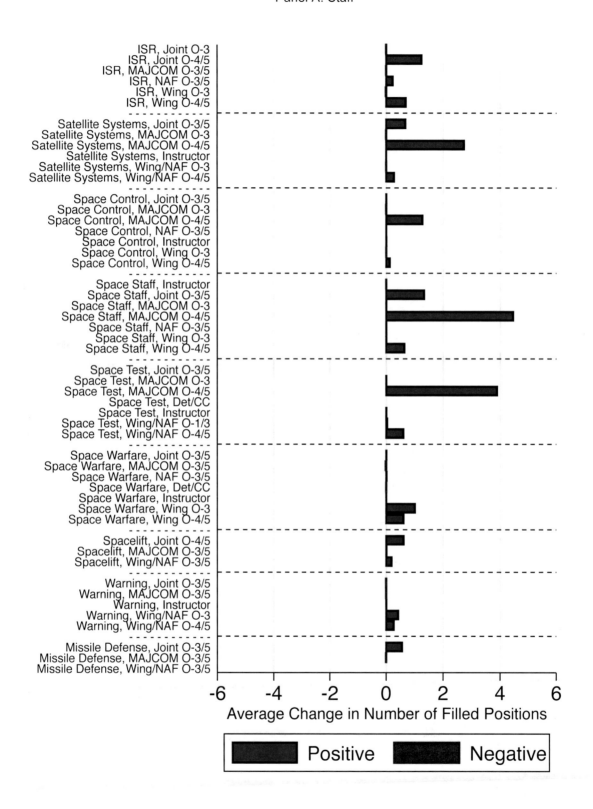

Panel B: Operations

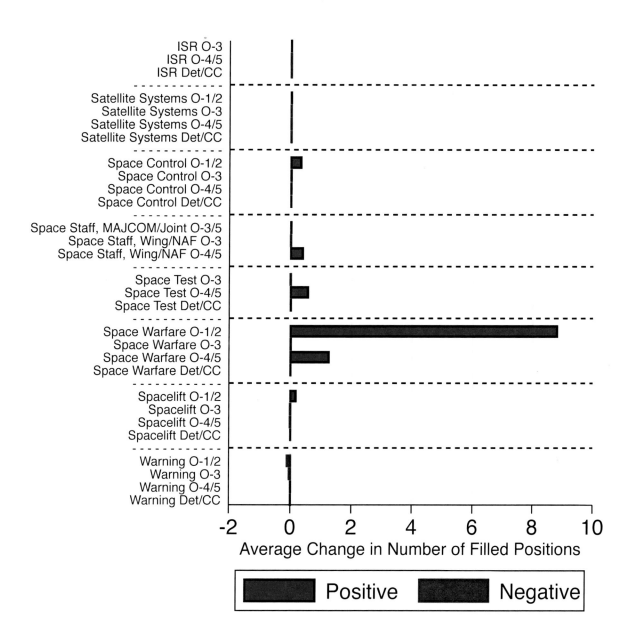

Panel C: Acquisition

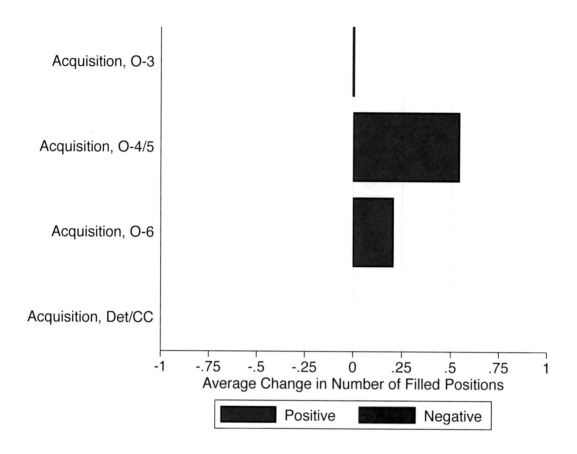

Given existing fill priorities, the distribution of positions in job categories, grade structure, and retention patterns, the MCM indicates that manning for only a few types of jobs would be affected by a significant reduction (50 percent) in the number of IR positions that must be filled by 13S officers. The positions freed up by reducing IRs will, in the steady state, go in general to O-4/5 staff positions, particularly those that are priority-fill positions, such as the space staff MAJCOM O-4/5 position, the Space Test O-4/5 position, and other MAJCOM-level staff positions. To some extent, reducing IRs may also allow above-grade fills of lower-priority positions, as the Space Warfare O-1/2 example demonstrates.

Effects on Individuals

To this point, we have focused on the effects of IRs from a career field perspective, examining the effect that IRs have had on the fill rates of different positions. In this section, we examine the effect of IRs on the careers of individual officers.

The space officer career field manager and career field representatives at AFSPC hypothesized that the requirement for their officers to serve in IR positions was negatively impacting the functional diversity and the operational depth of their officers. To better understand how frequently this hypothesis is realized in officer career paths, we first studied the extent to which changes in IRs affect the diversity of officer experience, focusing on individuals who have advanced to the O-5 level and beyond. Next, we examined the effect of IRs on the number of operations tours that officers were assigned to during their careers, again studying O-5s. Finally, we looked closely at individuals filling IR positions in the baseline scenario, and examined how removing IRs influenced the types of positions those officers would fill.

Retention Patterns for Officers with Different Types of IR Experiences

Because academic, operations, and recruiting IR experiences are sometimes perceived to make officers less competitive for senior-level positions, having a "bad IR" experience (being assigned to an IR position that ultimately hurts an officer's career) may also have a negative effect on retention. In Figure 3.13, we plot the survival curve of individuals that had "good IR" experiences—namely, IR experiences in functional command and senior leader support (in blue)—against the survival curve of officers that had "bad IR" experiences (in red). Panel A shows the results of this exercise for the baseline scenario and Panel B for the 50-percent IR reduction scenario.

Two main findings emerge from these results. First, individuals who have "bad IR" experiences tend to have lower retention than individuals with "good IR" experiences, with the biggest changes in retention coming after the seventh year of service, when officers are promoted to O-4 and become eligible for many IR positions. Second, under the 50-percent IR reduction scenario, the differences in retention become less significant. This is presumably because there are fewer "bad IR" positions under this scenario, and hence less of an opportunity for these positions to adversely affect officer careers.

Figure 3.13. Retention Patterns for Officers with Different Types of IR Experiences

Panel A: Baseline Scenario   Panel B: 50-Percent IR Reduction

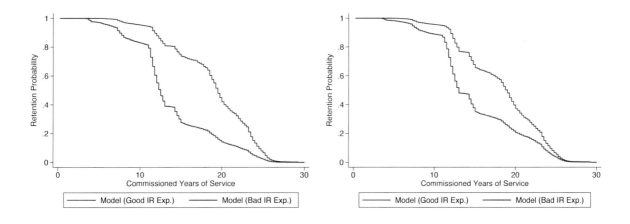

Diversity of Officer Experiences

To understand how IRs affect the diversity of officer experiences, we coded jobs into one of 11 experience areas: (1) acquisition, (2) IR jobs, (3) space control, (4) ISR, (5) spacelift, (6) missile defense, (7) satellite systems, (8) space staff, (9) space test, (10) space warfare, and (11) space warning. Then, for every officer who achieved at least the grade of O-5, we calculated the share of that officer's career spent in each of the experience areas. In the following equation, p_j denotes the fraction of an officer's career spent in experience area j. To measure the diversity of experiences, we used the following index:

$$D = 1 - \sum_j p_j{}^2.$$

This index, D, measures the probability that two randomly selected years in an officer's career were spent in different experience areas. The index ranges from 0 to 1, and as D increases, the officer's diversity of experiences also increases. At the extreme, $p_j = 1$ for some experience area j, so that $D = 0$, meaning that the officer spent his entire career in a single experience area.

We calculated D separately for each officer in the model. Figure 3.14 plots a histogram of the index across officers in the baseline scenario (Panel A) and under the 50-percent IR reduction scenario (Panel B). Generally, reducing IRs has little impact on the distribution of the diversity of officer experiences. Although officers tend to have slightly more diverse experiences under the IR reduction scenario, on average, the two distributions are quite similar. However, there are more officers who specialize in the 50-percent IR reduction scenario, with big increases in the left tail of the distribution (0.2–0.4).

Figure 3.14. Experience Diversity Index, O-5+ Officers

Panel A: Baseline Scenario   Panel B: 50-Percent IR Reduction

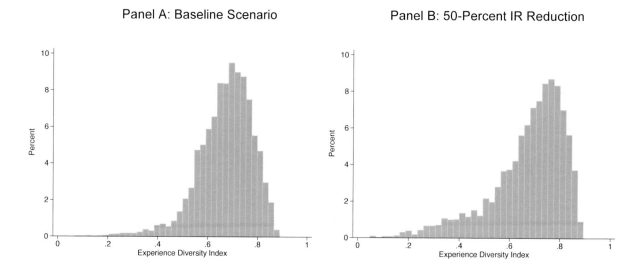

Number of Operational Positions

For O-5 officers, we also calculated the number of operational positions to which they had been assigned by the time they reached the O-5 grade. Figure 3.15 presents a histogram of the number of operational positions officers held during careers in the baseline scenario (Panel A) and under the 50-percent IR reduction scenario (Panel B).

Figure 3.15. Distribution of the Number of Operational Positions in a Career, O-5+ Officers

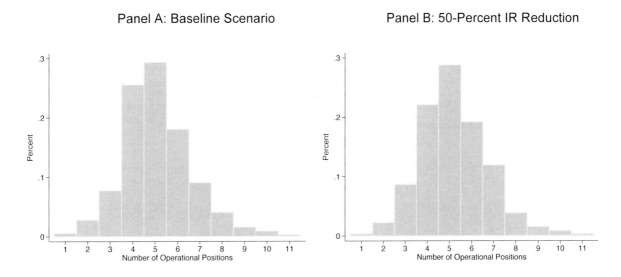

SOURCE: Authors' calculations.

In general, we find that the reduced IR scenario tends to increase the number of operational positions held by O-5 officers over the course of their careers. However, the average effect is small; the increase is only about 0.13 positions, on average. The biggest change is the reduction in the number of officers who had four operations positions; this mass in the distribution is now distributed in the right tail of Figure 3.15, Panel B. However, these effects are small, and IRs do not appear to substantially prevent 13S officers from obtaining operational experience.

Counterfactuals: How Do IRs Affect Individual Career Histories

In this final subsection, we turn to the question of what would have happened to officer career histories if those individuals were not filling IR positions. To do so, we again compare officer experiences for the baseline and 50-percent IR reduction scenarios. In the baseline scenario, we identify individuals who (1) had been promoted to O-5 status and (2) had noncareer-oriented IR assignments at some point in their career history. We then look at the career histories of those same individuals in the 50-percent IR reduction scenario and the differences in their career paths.

Figure 3.16 illustrates these comparisons for a small set of positions: detachment commanders and joint staff. The blue bars plot the percentage of our sample of officers that filled detachment commander positions and joint staff positions, while the gray bars plot the same percentages under the 50-percent IR reduction scenario. The results show that more of the officers who were assigned to IR positions would have become detachment commanders and assigned to a joint staff if there were fewer IR positions to fill. In the baseline model, less than 2 percent of O-5 officers who had baseline IR experience become detachment commanders, but when we reduce IR positions by 50 percent, the number jumps to more than 10 percent. A similar increase, but smaller in magnitude, happens for officers filling joint staff positions. This is evidence that IR experiences may adversely affect officer careers; if officers had not been assigned to IR jobs, some of them could have gone on to more important positions in the 13S career field.

At this point, it is worth reiterating that the model is not well suited to study individual behavior or characteristics, as all the "individuals" in the model are simulated and all of these simulated officers are of equal quality. Nevertheless, this analysis suggests important effects on individual officer careers.

Figure 3.16. Counterfactual Changes in Positions Filled for Officers with Baseline IR Experience: Baseline vs. 50-Percent IR Reduction

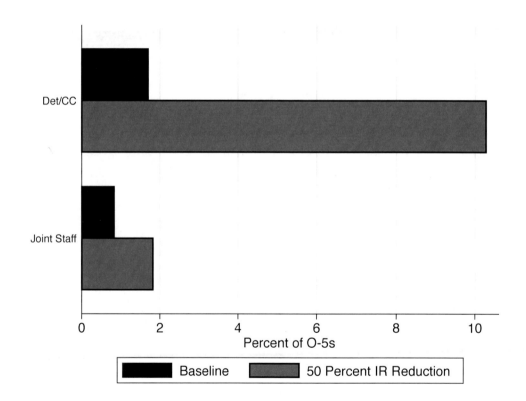

4. Conclusions and Recommendations

In this report, we have calibrated RAND's MCM and analyzed its outputs to assess the impact of IRs on a variety of outcomes for the space officer career field, both for the career field as a whole and for individual officers in the field.

Effects of IRs on the Space Career Field

Generally, we find that the fill rates of most space jobs would not be affected by reductions in the total number of IRs allocated to the space career field. The highest-priority (must-fill) career field positions would nearly always be filled, even if the space career field was required to fill more IR positions than is the case today. If fewer IRs were assigned to the career field, the biggest effect on fill rates would occur for slightly lower-priority jobs (those with slightly less priority than IR positions), particularly staff jobs at the grade of O-4. Jobs with lower priority than IR jobs often require grades and experiences that are inapplicable to IR positions, so these jobs would be unaffected by a change in IRs. Taken together, this evidence suggests that IRs have a substantial numerical effect on space career field manning overall, but the effect on the career field occurs only for certain types of space officer positions. If the number of IR positions assigned to the space career field were reduced, the positions most likely to experience higher fill rates would be action officers at MAJCOM and Headquarters Air Force staffs, where position vacancies would be most obvious to space senior leaders.

Effects of IRs on Space Officer Careers

The experiences of individual officers in the space career field are often used as examples of the negative effects of IRs on officer careers, such as effects on operational depth, diversity of experience across the space enterprise, and career advancement. Our review of the simulated officers in the MCM shows little evidence of these negative outcomes. From an individual perspective, we do not find much evidence that IRs affect the distribution of experience diversity or of the number of operational tours filled by officers. We do find, however, that many individuals who were assigned to IR positions would have done very different things during their careers were it not for their IR assignments. IRs may have positive or negative effects on officers' development and career progression. Because of these potential effects, those involved in officer assignments must be attentive to the careers of individual officers in subspecialties that need particular operational experiences and those with the potential for senior staff and command positions. They also need to be attentive to situations where IRs offer experiences and competencies that are different from those of space jobs but are of similar value.

Recommendations

While IRs do divert manpower that could be used to fill space officer positions, IRs do not compete with all types of space positions for officers. Therefore, IR effects on the career field could be lessened by careful management at the appropriate level of detail in the following areas.

- **Increasing the fidelity of the priorities for space jobs and ensuring space officer assignments are made based on these priorities.** Our analysis of IR effects at the career field and individual levels reveals the importance of prioritizing jobs. The space career field manager should consider creating a prioritization scheme with more levels (similar perhaps to the *must-fill*; *priority-fill, high*; *priority-fill, low;* and *entitlement-fill* ratings used in our analysis). This will help ensure that positions that now fall just outside of the top priority are more accurately reflected among the highest-priority positions. The 96 jobs we identified in our analysis may be a starting point for finer granularity. Top-to-bottom career field visibility of these priorities—from space senior leaders to the space assignment team—will also help ensure that all high-priority positions are filled.

- **Carefully selecting IR jobs for space officers.** For some space officers, IRs may have some degree of impact on diversity and depth of operational experience and represent lost opportunities. Since the 13S career field likely will continue to staff IR positions, we recommend that the space officer assignment team at AFPC, which is responsible for selecting the specific IR positions that space officers fill, take care in selection. The assignment team should seek IR positions that provide officers with experiences and competencies to enhance and complement their space expertise, rather than positions for which officers might be likely to volunteer. For example, operations staff officer (AFSC 16GX) positions that relate to space operations in a joint environment or planning and programming (16RX) positions that prepare officers to advocate for space systems and operations resources should be sought out, not avoided.

- **Continuing to maintain and possibly expanding the use and management of the Space Experience Code**. This code was an invaluable input to the modeling for this study. Continuing to accurately track the experiences of space officers within their career field is crucial to future career field analyses. By identifying the SPECs of individual officers, we were able to extrapolate the SPEC for each space authorization and develop a list of space jobs at a level above individual positions. AFSPC should consider extending SPEC use, including labeling each space authorization with a SPEC for future job-level analyses. In addition, we recommend that AF/A1 investigate the development of a similar standardized coding scheme that could be used by all officer career fields; analysis conducted using such a coding scheme would make a valuable contribution to many policy decisions across the Air Force personnel community.

The use of the MCM and the resulting analysis presented in this report are a first step toward understanding the impact of IRs on the space career field. Future work could examine the impact on the career field of changing the priority of space career positions and changing policies for filling IRs. The methodology can be readily used to study the impact of IRs on other career fields as well. We recommend that future work evaluate the impact of IRs on multiple career fields to determine which career fields have the most to gain from an improved IR selection and allocation process.

Appendix. Statistics on Jobs in Model

In Table A.1, we present statistics on jobs in the model, based on FY 2001–2014 personnel data. These statistics calculate, for every employment period, the number and percentage of officers who had different types of IR experiences. These statistics were used to code encouragements, discouragements, requirements, and disallowances in the logic of the MCM assignment model, as explained in Chapter Two.

Table A.1. Previous IR Experiences: Statistics on Employment Periods

Job Title	Code	Number of Employment Periods	Academic, Accessions, and Recruiting IR Experience		Functional Command and Senior Leader Support IR Experience		Operations IR Experience	
			N	%	N	%	N	%
Acquisition, O-3	ACQ3	85	2	2.4	2	2.4	1	1.2
Acquisition, O-4/5	ACQ4	149	14	9.4	10	6.7	11	7.4
Acquisition, O-6	ACQ6	16	2	12.5	2	12.5	2	12.5
Acquisition, Det/CC	ACQC	12	1	8.3	2	16.7	0	0
Ops, Space Control O-1/2	OCON1	113	0	0	0	0	0	0
Ops, Space Control O-3	OCON3	502	12	2.4	9	1.8	9	1.8
Ops, Space Control O-4/5	OCON4	267	18	6.7	23	8.6	16	6
Ops, Space Control Det/CC	OCONC	83	1	1.2	17	20.5	11	13.3
Staff, Space Control, Joint O-3/5	SCOJ4	28	0	0	7	25	1	3.6
Staff, Space Control, MAJCOM O-3	SCOM3	48	0	0	0	0	0	0
Staff, Space Control, MAJCOM O-4/5	SCOM4	216	12	5.6	19	8.8	19	8.8
Staff, Space Control, NAF O-3/5	SCON4	15	1	6.7	1	6.7	1	6.7
Staff, Space Control, Instructor	SCONT	23	0	0	1	4.3	0	0
Staff, Space Control, Wing O-3	SCOW3	49	0	0	1	2	0	0
Staff, Space Control, Wing O-4/5	SCOW4	118	6	5.1	13	11	11	9.3
Ops, ISR O-3	OISR3	167	3	1.8	2	1.2	2	1.2
Ops, ISR O-4/5	OISR4	131	7	5.3	17	13	10	7.6
Ops, ISR Det/CC	OISRC	51	1	2	21	41.2	4	7.8

48

Job Title	Code	Number of Employment Periods	Academic, Accessions, and Recruiting IR Experience		Functional Command and Senior Leader Support IR Experience		Operations IR Experience	
			N	%	N	%	N	%
Staff, ISR, Joint O-3	SISJ3	14	0	0	1	7.1	0	0
Staff, ISR, Joint O-4/5	SISJ4	53	3	5.7	5	9.4	6	11.3
Staff, ISR, MAJCOM O-3/5	SISM4	54	4	7.4	7	13	3	5.6
Staff, ISR, NAF O-3/5	SISN4	2	0	0	0	0	0	0
Staff, ISR, Wing O-3	SISW3	21	1	4.8	1	4.8	0	0
Staff, ISR, Wing O-4/5	SISW4	93	8	8.6	17	18.3	16	17.2
Ops, Spacelift O-1/2	OLFT1	173	1	0.6	0	0	0	0
Ops, Spacelift O-3	OLFT3	399	14	3.5	4	1	11	2.8
Ops, Spacelift O-4/5	OLFT4	229	18	7.9	28	12.2	24	10.5
Ops, Spacelift Det/CC	OLFTC	60	3	5	18	30	13	21.7
Staff, Spacelift, Joint O-4/5	SLFJ4	9	0	0	0	0	1	11.1
Staff, Spacelift, MAJCOM O-3/5	SLFM4	92	2	2.2	3	3.3	6	6.5
Staff, Spacelift, Wing/NAF O-3/5	SLFW4	34	0	0	1	2.9	4	11.8
Ops, Satellite Systems O-1/2	OSAT1	563	2	0.4	0	0	1	0.2
Ops, Satellite Systems O-3	OSAT3	872	29	3.3	10	1.1	8	0.9
Ops, Satellite Systems O-4/5	OSAT4	292	18	6.2	21	7.2	21	7.2
Ops, Satellite Systems Det/CC	OSATC	125	12	9.6	22	17.6	19	15.2
Staff, Satellite Systems, Joint O-3/5	SSAJ4	30	5	16.7	3	10	0	0
Staff, Satellite Systems, MAJCOM O-3	SSAM3	43	0	0	0	0	2	4.7
Staff, Satellite Systems, MAJCOM O-4/5	SSAM4	137	15	10.9	17	12.4	11	8
Staff, Satellite Systems, Instructor	SSATT	122	2	1.6	0	0	1	0.8
Staff, Satellite Systems, Wing/NAF O-3	SSAW3	46	1	2.2	1	2.2	0	0
Staff, Satellite Systems, Wing/NAF O-4/5	SSAW4	84	5	6	8	9.5	5	6
Ops, Space Staff, MAJCOM/Joint O-3/5	OSTFJ	62	7	11.3	5	8.1	6	9.7
Ops, Space Staff, Wing/NAF O-3	OSTW3	51	2	3.9	1	2	0	0
Ops, Space Staff, Wing/NAF O-4/5	OSTW4	77	6	7.8	10	13	11	14.3
Staff, Space Staff, Instructor	SSTFT	16	2	12.5	2	12.5	2	12.5

Job Title	Code	Number of Employment Periods	Academic, Accessions, and Recruiting IR Experience		Functional Command and Senior Leader Support IR Experience		Operations IR Experience	
			N	%	N	%	N	%
Staff, Space Staff, Joint O-3/5	SSTJ4	252	29	11.5	38	15.1	40	15.9
Staff, Space Staff, MAJCOM O-3	SSTM3	124	3	2.4	5	4	4	3.2
Staff, Space Staff, MAJCOM O-4/5	SSTM4	767	79	10.3	112	14.6	106	13.8
Staff, Space Staff, NAF O-3/5	SSTN4	63	2	3.2	4	6.3	4	6.3
Staff, Space Staff, Wing O-3	SSTW3	94	2	2.1	2	2.1	2	2.1
Staff, Space Staff, Wing O-4/5	SSTW4	463	43	9.3	68	14.7	59	12.7
Ops, Space Test O-3	OTST3	180	9	5	0	0	3	1.7
Ops, Space Test O-4/5	OTST4	94	6	6.4	8	8.5	7	7.4
Ops, Space Test Det/CC	OTSTC	32	2	6.2	5	15.6	2	6.2
Staff, Space Test, Joint O-3/5	STSJ4	49	4	8.2	2	4.1	4	8.2
Staff, Space Test, MAJCOM O-3	STSM3	97	4	4.1	1	1	2	2.1
Staff, Space Test, MAJCOM O-4/5	STSM4	240	24	10	15	6.2	28	11.7
Staff, Space Test, Det/CC	STSTC	35	3	8.6	7	20	10	28.6
Staff, Space Test, Instructor	STSTT	142	9	6.3	4	2.8	2	1.4
Staff, Space Test, Wing/NAF O-1/3	STSW3	143	5	3.5	1	0.7	5	3.5
Staff, Space Test, Wing/NAF O-4/5	STSW4	218	23	10.6	12	5.5	24	11
Ops, Space Warfare O-1/2	OWAR1	52	0	0	0	0	0	0
Ops, Space Warfare O-3	OWAR3	340	7	2.1	3	0.9	5	1.5
Ops, Space Warfare O-4/5	OWAR4	377	34	9	25	6.6	33	8.8
Ops, Space Warfare Det/CC	OWARC	10	0	0	1	10	2	20
Staff, Space Warfare, Joint O-3/5	SWAJ4	48	6	12.5	5	10.4	3	6.2
Staff, Space Warfare, MAJCOM O-3/5	SWAM4	215	20	9.3	18	8.4	29	13.5
Staff, Space Warfare, NAF O-3/5	SWAN4	48	3	6.2	7	14.6	1	2.1
Staff, Space Warfare, Det/CC	SWARC	15	1	6.7	2	13.3	2	13.3
Staff, Space Warfare, Instructor	SWART	9	2	22.2	0	0	0	0
Staff, Space Warfare, Wing O-3	SWAW3	125	1	0.8	6	4.8	2	1.6
Staff, Space Warfare, Wing O-4/5	SWAW4	246	14	5.7	26	10.6	22	8.9

Job Title	Code	Number of Employment Periods	Academic, Accessions, and Recruiting IR Experience		Functional Command and Senior Leader Support IR Experience		Operations IR Experience	
			N	%	N	%	N	%
Ops, Warning O-1/2	OWRN1	271	5	1.8	0	0	0	0
Ops, Warning O-3	OWRN3	379	16	4.2	5	1.3	5	1.3
Ops, Warning O-4/5	OWRN4	269	21	7.8	27	10	23	8.6
Ops, Warning Det/CC	OWRNC	69	4	5.8	18	26.1	11	15.9
Staff, Warning, Joint O-3/5	SWRJ4	15	1	6.7	1	6.7	1	6.7
Staff, Warning, MAJCOM O-3/5	SWRM4	111	13	11.7	4	3.6	8	7.2
Staff, Warning, Instructor	SWRNT	78	4	5.1	0	0	1	1.3
Staff, Warning, Wing/NAF O-3	SWRW3	38	0	0	0	0	1	2.6
Staff, Warning, Wing/NAF O-4/5	SWRW4	42	12	28.6	5	11.9	2	4.8
Staff, Missile Defense, Joint O-3/5	SMIJ4	35	4	11.4	8	22.9	5	14.3
Staff, Missile Defense, MAJCOM O-3/5	SMIM4	100	10	10	13	13	11	11
Staff, Missile Defense, Wing/NAF O-3/5	SMIW4	57	3	5.3	3	5.3	4	7

References

Air Force Doctrine Document 3-14, "Space Operations," 2012.

Air Force Personnel Center, Authorized Manpower Master Files (MPW). Accessed on September 1, 2014.

Beary, Daniel, Owen C. Brown, Chris Crawford, Jack "Jay" D. Fulmer II, and Gordon Roesler, "Leading into the Future: Creating the Cadre of Space Professionals," *High Frontier: The Journal for Space and Cyberspace Professionals*, Vol. 7, No. 4, 2007, pp. 21–28.

Harrington, Lisa M., Kathleen Reedy, Paul Emslie, Darrell D. Jones, and Tara L. Terry, *Air Force Institutional Requirements: Opportunities for Improving the Efficiency of Sourcing, Managing, and Manning Corporate Requirements*, Santa Monica, Calif.: RAND Corporation, RR-1596-AF, 2017. As of July 2017:
http://www.rand.org/pubs/research_reports/RR1596.html

Headquarters U.S. Air Force, Directorate of Military Force Policy, Force Management and Enterprise Readiness Analysis Division, "Cumulative Continuation Rates for 13S Officers by Commissioned Years of Service," data files, 2015.

Hutto, James C., "Developing Space Professionals Crucial to Critical Wartime Roles," *High Frontier: The Journal for Space and Cyberspace Professionals*, Vol. 1, No. 1, pp. 8–11, 2004.

Nataraj, Shanthi, Christopher Guo, Philip Hall-Partyka, Susan M. Gates, and Douglas Yeung, *Options for Department of Defense Total Workforce Supply and Demand Analysis: Potential Approaches and Available Data Sources*, Santa Monica, Calif.: RAND Corporation, RR-543-OSD, 2014. As of September 2, 2016:
http://www.rand.org/pubs/research_reports/RR543.html

O'Neill, Kevin, *Sustaining the US Air Force's Force Support Career Field Through Officer Workforce Planning*, Santa Monica, Calif.: RAND Corporation, RGSD-302, 2012. As of September 2, 2016:
http://www.rand.org/pubs/rgs_dissertations/RGSD302.html

Payton, Gary E., "Air Force Space Acquisition," *High Frontier: The Journal for Space and Cyberspace Professionals*, Vol. 6, No. 1, 2009, pp. 3–5.

Schirmer, Peter, *Computer Simulation of General and Flag Officer Management: Model Description and Results*, Santa Monica, Calif.: RAND Corporation, TR-702-OSD, 2009. As of September 2, 2016:
http://www.rand.org/pubs/technical_reports/TR702.html

Schirmer, Peter, Harry J. Thie, Margaret C. Harrell, and Michael S. Tseng, *Challenging Time in DOPMA: Flexible and Contemporary Military Officer Management*, Santa Monica, Calif.: RAND Corporation, MG-451-OSD, 2006. As of September 2, 2016:
http://www.rand.org/pubs/monographs/MG451.html